SOULS BEHIND THE BADGE

SOULS
BEHIND THE
BADGE

The Real World of Policing —
An Insider's View

WAYNE RYAN

© 2013 by Wayne Ryan

Cover & book design: Natalie Olsen (kisscutdesign.com)
Author photo: Laird Allan of D. Laird Allan Photography
Editor: Suzanne Paschall

Produced by Indie Ink Publishing's Story Incorporated
(www.storyincorporated.com)
#220, 220 20th Street West
Saskatoon, SK, Canada S7M 0W9
T 888.438.1343

Printed in Canada by Houghton Boston
First edition: September, 2013
ISBN: 978-1-927714-00-3

Also available in e-book form
ISBN: 978-1-927714-01-0

Library and Archives Canada Cataloguing in Publication
Ryan, Wayne, 1954–, author
Souls behind the badge: the real world of policing, an insider's view /
Wayne Ryan.

Issued in print and electronic formats.
ISBN 978-1-927714-00-3 (pbk.). — ISBN 978-1-927714-01-0 (pdf)

1. Police — Canada. 2. Police psychology — Canada. 3. Police-community
relations — Canada. 4. Law enforcement — Canada. I. Title.

HV8157.R83 2013 363.20971 C2013-904451-5
C2013-904452-3

This book is dedicated the men and women in law enforcement who have made the ultimate sacrifice and paid the ultimate price.

This is a special dedication to Royal Canadian Mounted Police officer, Constable Adrian Oliver, who died in the line of duty on Nov 13, 2012 at 5:00 AM less than eight blocks from my home. His partner, brother and father are all serving members with the Royal Canadian Mounted Police.

Adrian has been described by both peers and supervisors as an outstanding police officer.

In honor of his sacrifice, I wrote this poem:

Constable Adrian Oliver

A young man dead too early
Two families bound in grief
One family loved for many years
The other's time too brief
One family, wife & brother,
And parents loved so deep
The other family Mounties
Together both will weep
For Adrian was many things
A brother, son and friend
And though they mourn his early death
His memory will not end
He gave his life protecting all
And all is what he gave
His place secure in Heaven
Where God protects the brave

Disclaimer

In writing this book, the author has drawn on his own experience as a 21-year veteran of the RCMP as well as on the collective experience of many others. This book contains stories and cases that are based on actual events; however in many cases the author has changed names or locations in respect of privacy regulations or to protect the privacy of individuals or police departments.

In some cases the author has attempted to recreate events and actions from verbal accounts as relayed to him by others and has relied on this anecdotal evidence and upon his imperfect memory of such. In a few instances, the author has used details of several different events and merged them into a composite story line for the purposes of supporting an opinion or thought process of the author.

When the author alludes to a study or report, it is as a lay person and will only bear the weight of his own interpretation. It is also quite evident that this book contains many personal opinions of the author and they are just that, personal opinions. Any errors of fact, any omissions and all opinions are the sole responsibility of the author and not that of the publishing consultant, the RCMP or any other person or agency unless expressly stated otherwise.

CONTENTS

Acknowledgements

The writing of a book is never an individual effort and in my case that statement could never be truer. You see truth be told, I'm not really a professional writer and the process of turning thoughts into words and words onto paper and that paper into a book required many helping hands!

I'd like to start out by thanking my wonderful publishing consultant and very patient editor, Suzanne Paschall at Indie Ink Publishing's Story Incorporated. I do not exaggerate when I say that, without her, this book would simply not have happened. Her guidance, experience and incredible dedication took this book from a concept to reality and I owe her a huge debt of thanks! The construction of the book and the awesome cover design was the work of Natalie Olsen and her company, Kisscut Design and I owe her many, many thanks for her amazing creativity. In so many cases a book "is" judged by its cover and with Natalie at the helm that is a "good" thing!

Thanks go to Mike Chicoine, Terry Ryan and Blair Ryan for previewing this book and offering not only encouragement but constructive criticism and genuine feedback, all of which was greatly appreciated.

A huge acknowledgement to my many friends in law enforcement who have, over the years, provided much of the content in this book by way of stories told, actions taken and for the many hours of frank conversations, honest opinions and, in many cases, the baring of souls. You, my friends, are 'why' I wrote this book!

To my children, Dan and Christine I say thank you for your love and support throughout this journey. Your suggestions and input were much appreciated and your dear old dad loves you to death!

And last, but I assure you not least, my beautiful wife Helene, without whom this book would truly not have been published. It was her, who, when this book was simply a pile of paper, literally forced me to send it around to publishing companies. She was the first to read the initial manuscript, the first to offer editing suggestions and in truth, the first to see its potential as a marketable book. Simply another several items which must be added to the very long list of reasons why I am so blessed to call her my wife!

MY STORY

If the teller of the tale has no tale to tell,
then the reader of the tale is unlikely to dwell!

I grew up in rural Saskatchewan and wrote my first letter to the RCMP when I was 13 years old. Upon graduating high school, I attended the University of Saskatchewan where I enrolled in a three-year Bachelor of Arts degree program. I graduated with my BA and went on to join the force in 1975.

Much has been written about the RCMP training facility in Regina Saskatchewan, known and remembered with varying degrees of fondness as "Depot." This is where young men and women were sent to become "Mounties," and for those who went on to graduate, it would forever become a part of who they were. Stories about Depot were legend and its impact can best be understood if one listens closely when veteran RCMP officers, long retired, gather together and tell stories and share laughs about their time at Depot.

After graduating from Depot I was posted to Vancouver Island where I spent five years in uniform patrol duties. In 1981, I was transferred to Prince Rupert Detachment where I spent one year in uniform patrol duties, one year on the drug section and two years in the plainclothes GIS (Detective) section. It was there that I had my first real experience investigating homicides and major crimes. From that point I knew what I wanted to do as a police officer.

When my tour of northern service ended, I asked for and was granted a transfer to Surrey Detachment. My reasoning was simple. I'd had the opportunity to work on a few serious crime investigations while on plain-clothes duties in Prince Rupert and discovered that I was intrigued and challenged by the complexities and the demands of major criminal investigations. Since Surrey was, and still is, the largest RCMP Detachment in Canada and experienced all of the serious crime typical to a large urban center, I thought, if you want to investigate major crimes, go where the work is! Subsequently I worked for about 1 year in uniform patrol duties and was then transferred to the Surrey Serious Crimes Unit.

I went on to spend the next 10 years investigating all the major crimes that occur in large, urban centers. I estimate that I took part in over 80 homicide investigations, many as the main investigator or as one of the peripheral investigators. During that time we used all available investigative techniques such as wire taps, undercover operations, surveillance, informants, forensics and DNA and arrested hundreds of suspects in major crimes.

In 1988 I became one of two hostage negotiators at Surrey Detachment and had an opportunity to work with the Emergency Response Team on many hostage and barricaded persons investigations. In 1988 I was promoted to corporal and remained on Surrey Serious Crimes Unit. It was also in that year that I got married. It was short lived and we were divorced a year later. In 1990 I met my current wife who had two children and we were married in 1992.

It was at this point that my personal goals began to change course. I had been on major crimes for seven years and the hours, the stress and the things I had seen and done were beginning to take their toll. I now had a family to consider and suddenly discovered that there was more to life than police work. In 1995 I was promoted to the rank of Sergeant and, while remaining at Surrey Detachment, moved from Serious Crimes to the non-commissioned officer (NCO) in charge of property crimes. But my focus had changed and I knew that I needed a change too. In 1996, with many reservations and a heavy heart, I resigned from the RCMP and immediately began my new career, alongside my wife, in real estate.

Since I have referred to the RCMP, I should explain to those who don't know, just what the RCMP is. It is the acronym for Royal Canadian Mounted Police, who are the national police force of Canada. The duties and functions of the RCMP are extremely broad based. If one were to compare the RCMP to their counterparts in the United States you would have to take the Federal Bureau of Investigation (FBI), the Drug Enforcement Agency (DEA), Alcohol Tobacco and Firearms (ATF), Homeland Security, the Secret Service, the Immigration Department, the State Police, the County Sheriff and the City Police, roll them into one large organization, and you would have the RCMP!

To date, I have maintained many friendships with current and retired RCMP members and am a member of the RCMP Veterans' Association. It's been said, "Once a police officer always a police officer," and while I'm not sure if that is true or not, certainly many of the values, characteristics, attitudes and feelings remain the same.

I am proud beyond words to have been a member of the select few who have served as police officers and speaking personally, if you were to scratch this particular civilian, he'd still bleed a little bit of blue.

INTRODUCTION

Goals without purpose or purpose without goals...
both are doomed to failure!

The public have long been fascinated with law enforcement and the men and women who work in it. Since 1952, when Sgt. Joe Friday first appeared in the TV police series *Dragnet*, there have been countless TV shows, novels, memoirs and movies about policing. Still today police oriented stories are prolific in the Television and Movie industries. With few exceptions, these shows and movies have been fiction or carefully scripted docu-fiction and even the fact-based literature has been heavily structured toward memoirs, anecdotes and stories about policing.

I wanted to write something that tried to *explain* policing, to give people an opportunity to see into the real world of law enforcement — to expel the myths, reveal the truths and identify the challenges. I wanted to explain how and why police officers make the decisions they do and why sometimes those decisions are wrong. To discuss why and when police use force, how it can go wrong and the significant impact of media reporting on public perceptions and expectations. I wanted to speak frankly about sexual harassment, bullying, gender bias and other allegations of police misconduct. And I very much wanted the reader to understand the human aspect of policing — how police officers are affected by the things they see and do and the magnificent job they do in spite of all the challenges. In essence, I wanted to show people the true, visceral, no holds barred and behind the scenes story of law enforcement as seen through the eyes of a police officer.

To do this I have drawn on my own experience as a 21-year veteran of the RCMP as well as the collective experience of many others. Many of the observations and conclusions I arrive at are based on my own personal experiences, attitudes or opinions and are largely anecdotal in nature. When I allude to a study or report, it is as a lay person and it will only bear the weight of my own interpretation. Wherever I have discussed specific cases or incidents it has been as a tool to explain a response, a feeling, a thought process or an example. In some cases, I have changed names and generalized locations. Unless otherwise stated, all of the opinions expressed are my own and I wish to make it clear that I am in no way a spokesperson for the RCMP or any other police department or agency.

Law enforcement is an honorable career and the vast majority of the men and women who are law enforcement officers are honorable people. I believe that truly and absolutely, but the point must be made that they are human beings and as such are subject to all the vagaries of human behavior. This is my attempt to introduce you to those humans — the *Souls Behind the Badge.*

The Soul Behind the Badge

The price is steep and the toll is high
And it's paid for you and me
It's paid by those Behind the Badge
To keep us safe and free

Behind the Badge is a lonely place
That few will ever know
A place of fear and darkness
Where you'll never need to go

The line is thin, and the walls are low
But they're manned both night and day
Behind the Badge they stand on guard
They keep us from harm's way

Behind the Badge a person stands
A mother, son or wife
A husband, daughter, father
Prepared to give their life

Yes, the toll is high and the price is steep
To keep us safe and free
So don't forget that Behind the Badge
Stands a soul like you and me

by Wayne Ryan

7

1

THE HUMAN FACTOR

*Police officers are also sons, daughters, husbands,
wives, fathers and mothers...lest we forget!*

What do we really see when we observe a police officer walking
down the street? When an officer issues us a traffic ticket? When
we watch them making arrests, handling a riot or attending an
accident? What are our perceptions and our expectations? Do we
resent or fear them as someone who has authority over us? Or do
we respect them as someone who maintains order and protects
us? Do we see a person or just a uniform? Who are these men
and women who walk among us?

First and foremost, police officers are people. Human beings
like the rest of us. They are the moms at the park playing with
their children, or the dads with their kids at the sports field.
They're that couple struggling to make car and mortgage pay-
ments. They're sons and daughters dealing with elderly parents,
and the husbands and wives juggling family and work schedules.
They may even be your neighbor down the street.

Police officers have all the same problems, issues, strengths
and weaknesses as the general public from which they come.
They are not immune to family or financial problems, substance
abuse, mental and physical health issues or any of the myriad of
issues that any other human being deals with. Nor are officers
immune to the same emotions that affect anyone else. The fact

that an officer must remain stoic in the face of pain and suffering does not for a moment mean they are unaffected, don't care or have no feelings.

Yes. It's in the job that we begin to notice the difference. Police work is a hard task master and the demands are high. Feelings and emotions may be the same, but every police officer must learn to put those emotions aside and present a resolute and professional demeanor.

In essence, they must learn to submerge at least a part of their human side without forsaking their humanity.

In truth, the nature of police work can have a high human cost and it's a cost paid by the individual officer. It's almost impossible to be an active police officer and not become somewhat desensitized. How can you spend a shift dealing with a seriously abused child and then show the necessary sensitivity and empathy when off duty to a spouse who has had an argument with a co-worker, or a child who has lost their homework, or a citizen who has had their bicycle stolen?

Intellectually, you may realize that the situation is important to them, but how do you make the emotional transition? This may be interpreted as a lack of caring or concern and can cause resentment and anger. It may well be one of the leading causes of divorce, which has been reported to be as high as 75% amongst police officers, and it certainly becomes another factor that can affect an officer's attitude, mood and performance and which can change from one day to the next.

In a given shift, an officer may be required to notify a family that their son or daughter has been killed by a drunk driver. Handled properly, this takes the compassion and empathy of a priest or trained counselor. An hour later the same officer may have to arrest an impaired driver who is abusive and uncooperative and he/she *must* find a way to compartmentalize those two very different duties and the very different emotional responses.

Later, in the same shift, the officer may have to intervene in a bar fight. Handled correctly, this may require physical courage and a strong, commanding approach. Even later, they may have to handle a dispute between two neighbors which, handled properly, may call for the mediation skills of a lawyer or judge. Counselor, enforcer and mediator...all in one short eight to 12 hour shift.

Can any one individual have *all* the skills that may be required? For example, you may well have an officer who is strong, decisive and commanding, but who struggles with sensitivity or empathy. Conversely, you may have an officer who is sensitive and empathetic, but who struggles with the ability to command or take charge of a critical situation.

Consider for a moment some of the qualities that might be present in the "*perfect*" police officer. Honesty, integrity, honor, compassion, empathy, commanding, decisiveness, tolerance, neutrality, lack of bias, hard-working, conscientious, fair, firm, courageous, cautious, and of course the list goes on. In fact, it's such a comprehensive and varied list that it would be literally impossible to find all of those qualities in any one individual.

This still might work if an officer's work environment, deployment or duties were constant, but that is simply not the case. Those factors vary considerably in any given shift and police officers don't get to pick and choose their assignments, or the calls they will attend. This of course means that officers find themselves dealing with situations which call for a different skill set or personality type than what they have and they simply must adapt to each call to the best of their abilities. Can any human being do this over and over and get it right every time? I sure couldn't, but most of the officers I ever knew and worked with did it as well as anyone could have.

The public, however, tends to have a much different understanding and expectation. They simply expect that every police officer should have all of the skills and abilities required to handle anything that occurs.

When a situation requiring decisive, commanding action is assigned to an officer whose personality and real strength and skill set is compassion and empathy and who simply does not have a strong, commanding style or ability, the public's reaction is invariably to be disappointed and unforgiving in their criticism.

Conversely, if a situation requiring compassion and empathy is assigned to an officer who is strong, decisive and commanding but simply does not have a compassionate or empathetic personality, again, the public will be disappointed and critical of the officer and the police department.

In some cases, supervisors can assign calls based on individual strengths and weakness but that would be rare and almost impossible to do with any regularity.

The point I'm trying to make is that we must remember that police officers are human beings with all the normal human traits. They will have individual strengths and individual weaknesses. They will have good days and bad days. They will disappoint. In spite of best efforts, officers will make mistakes and there will be human error. Some of these errors will be in judgment, some in behavior.

Individual police officers should be held accountable for their actions and decisions. There is little argument about that. We must, however, take care that we do not judge all officers by the actions of a few...that we don't judge an entire police department because a few have failed.

EXPERIENCE: THE GREAT TEACHER

While working uniform patrol duties in Prince Rupert, I was dispatched to a motor vehicle accident. Upon arrival, it appeared to be fairly minor in nature. One vehicle had been forced to stop suddenly, I don't recall exactly why, and the following vehicle had slammed into the rear end of it. The lead vehicle had been a sturdily built truck with reinforced bumpers and was still drivable. The other vehicle was a small compact and it was badly damaged in the front end.

I spoke briefly with both drivers. The truck driver was fine. The female driver of the second vehicle, while alert and ambulatory was complaining of chest pain. She stated that she had not been wearing her seatbelt and had hit her chest on the steering wheel. Acting on the safe side, we called an ambulance and she was taken to the hospital. Imagine my shock when we received news an hour later that she had died. A subsequent autopsy would show that the blow to the steering wheel had caused a fatal aortic rupture.

Later that same day, and prior to autopsy results, I was asked to return to the office to speak with someone regarding this accident. When I arrived, I found that it was the deceased's fiancé. I took him into a small, private office and began to answer his questions as best I could. The fiancé was a large man and as he sat there, he was clearly fighting his emotions. When I had answered his questions, he began to ask me how such a minor accident could have resulted in her death. I couldn't answer. He then started to become angry, seemingly at me. He got angrier and angrier and finally smashed his fist down onto a paper cup of coffee that was sitting on the table. The coffee exploded all over him, the table and me.

Partly out of shock, partly out of fear and partly out of pain, I quickly stood and asked him to leave the office. He immediately apologized and asked if he could stay and ask a few more questions. To my shame, I insisted that I could not tell him anything else and that he should leave. To this day it remains one of the things in my life that I would like the chance to do over. Certainly I know I'd have handled it much differently even just a few years later.

You see, I was a 25-year-old police officer who had never been married, had no children and grew up in a family of five boys. I simply did not have the empathetic skills or maturity to understand what had really transpired. This man had just lost a loved one. He was searching for answers that deep down he must have known I couldn't answer. But he had nowhere else to turn. His anger wasn't directed at me. It wasn't even real anger. I know now that it was simply an expression of his grief and pain. His hurt and the understandable search for a logical answer or reason where none existed. . .I wish I'd just gone and gotten him another cup of coffee.

2

EXPECTATION VS. REALITY

Disappointment occurs when expectation exceeds performance. The question then becomes: are expectations too high or is performance too low?

It's almost impossible to describe police work to someone who has never done it. It's an incredibly difficult job to do well and one that's not well understood by most. So what do we know and understand about policing? What is asked and expected of our police officers?

We ask police officers to confront danger so that danger does not confront us. We ask them to place themselves in harm's way so that harm will not befall us. We ask them to deal with society's failures, cruelty, evil, pain and suffering so that we do not have to deal with it, and we ask them to do all this while remaining within the confines of our laws and regulations. This is what we ask our police officers to do. . .what we *expect* them to do.

But let's examine what else we expect of our officers. We expect them to remain calm and controlled in the face of chaos. We expect them to be fearless and selfless when in harm's way, to be tolerant in the face of physical and emotional abuse and to remain unaffected by that constant exposure to cruelty, evil, pain and suffering. We want them to have the physical abilities of a young person and the wisdom of a senior, to be all-knowing and all seeing, patient and understanding, sensitive but strong. But what standards do we use by which to measure and compare?

Actually, most members of the public have very little significant contact with the police over the course of their lives. In fact, studies have shown that 95% of the general public forms their perceptions and expectations of the police from the mass media and the hundreds of TV police shows that have been aired over the years (Surette, 1998:197). There, officers tend to be portrayed in one of two manners. One is as the tough, driven, hard-drinking, hard-living cops who will break any and all rules to get the bad guy. The other portrayal is of the perfect cops who have all of the desired qualities. They're wise, courageous, tolerant and unaffected by the things they have to see and do. They can arrest suspects with a few deft moves, shoot to wound, never make a mistake and always solve the crime. This makes for great TV, but leaves an erroneous perception and places an impossible expectation on the officers doing the real job in the real world.

In almost every case, when expectations exceed the ability to perform, there will be disappointment.

Much is made of the fact that officers are "trained" to handle all of the situations they may encounter. Seriously? How do you train someone to "handle" seeing a child with a dozen cigarette burns on their body? How do you train someone to "handle" picking up body parts at a crime or accident scene? How do you train someone to "handle" the overwhelming grief of a parent who has lost a child to suicide or a violent crime? Consider for a moment what we do as a society when there is a mass shooting at a college or university. We rush counselors in to manage the grief and trauma of the witnesses and who would disagree with that? But consider that many of the police officers who have had to attend that same scene may be the same age or even younger than many of those college students. There simply is no "training" for this sort of thing. They just go on to another scene, possibly more emotionally difficult than the last.

We like to believe that a police officer is "trained" in martial arts or self-defense to a degree that allows him or her to make an arrest using minimal force and causing no injury to the suspect. Really? Ask a martial arts expert one day how many years of extensive training it would take to do that. Most officers receive approximately six months of training (see Chapter 19), a small portion of it devoted to self-defense. There is nothing pretty about a physical altercation between two or more adults and there is no way to make it look the way they do in the movies.

The same thing applies whenever the police are involved in any large, unusual or unique investigation. Because this type of investigation is quite rare, when one does occur there is much on the job learning and there are bound to be some procedural errors. Like other organizations, police try to learn from mistakes and success — in short, from experience.

There is no innate, God-given talent bestowed upon police officers that gives them the power or ability to make the right decision in every situation regardless of circumstance or experience.

CASE STUDY:
Pickton & Vancouver's missing women

In 2002, the RCMP and Vancouver Police Department launched a massive investigation into missing and murdered females. As the investigation unfolded, it became clear that it was the work of a serial killer and police were eventually lead to a pig farm owned and operated by Robert "Willie" Pickton. With dozens of missing women and almost no recovered bodies or remains, police began to suspect that Pickton had disposed of the bodies on his farm. Inspector Don Adams, a major crime inspector, who I knew personally to be one of the RCMP's most talented and competent investigators, was put in charge. So began the largest and most unique investigation in Canadian history.

In fact, it was such an unusual investigation, requiring police to excavate almost the entire farm and sift through tons and tons of earth for human remains, that nothing like it had been undertaken in North America. Officers were required to consult with investigators from agencies that had been involved with investigating war crimes and the mass graves found in Bosnia during the Civil War. In the end, after an investigation spanning several years, Pickton was charged with 26 counts of murder. He was ultimately convicted of six of these murders and sentenced to life in prison. Crown Counsel entered a stay of proceedings on the remaining 20 counts.

One can't even imagine the countless hours that officers spent away from their families. How many ball games, dance recitals, birthdays and anniversaries were missed? How many fast food meals were eaten hastily in wet, cold conditions. The stale coffee, the late hours. And always, the crushing pressure to get it right while traversing new and unknown territory.

In spite of this, the case generated considerable criticism of the police with the main complaints being that the victims had been marginalized by the police, that reports of missing women had not been investigated properly or at all and police had failed to recognize a pattern to the missing women complaints and thus had failed to apprehend the suspect sooner. While almost any large and complex investigation will result in mistakes being made, it is always worth reviewing the circumstances in a balanced and dispassionate manner to determine what criticism is warranted, what is not and how police departments might learn from mistakes and adopt changes or improvements to avoid similar mistakes in the future.

When discussing the accusation that police marginalized the victims, it's necessary to shed normal "politically correct" observations and speak frankly. The fact is that many of the victims were drug addicted sex trade workers from the down town east side of Vancouver. Intellectually, most people would agree that every life is valuable and equal under the eyes of God and the legal system. The question then arises as to how we, as a society, actually think and feel about this. To illustrate the point I'm making, let us consider several scenarios. When considering these, readers will have to be totally honest with themselves.

Issue #1: Bias

Take for example a gang member who is shot and killed during a drug dispute and compare his death to that of a young doctor who is shot and killed during a street robbery. While it can't be argued that the doctor's life was more valuable than the gang member's, I suspect that most people would intuitively feel that the doctor's death was the more tragic of the two. That the gang member had placed himself into danger by becoming involved with gangs and drug dealing and had perhaps even been the author of his own demise.

Another comparison would be a sex trade worker who is murdered while plying her trade as compared to the death of a university student walking home from class. Again, one simply cannot suggest that one's life was more important than the other's but, as in the prior example, most people will feel the death of the university student to be the more tragic. While I was not there and certainly can't say for sure, it would not be surprising to discover that some police officers would feel the same way.

Not that the sex trade worker's life was not important, but that the investigation of their death or disappearance was more of a routine matter. There is really no defense to this attitude other than to reiterate that police officers are simply normal human beings selected from the society in which they were raised and wouldn't necessarily be immune to the same biases and attitudes of the general public.

This is not to infer in any way that such investigations are conducted in an inferior manner because that would simply not be true. I have been a part of many investigations where the victim was involved in criminal behavior or had put themselves in harm's way because of lifestyle or other choices and in every case, the same resources, investigative techniques and efforts were put into the investigation. The differences, however, can be significant.

When the victim is involved with criminal activity, the general public is often somewhat apathetic and there may be a feeling that they and their loved ones are not at risk because they don't live that sort of lifestyle. There may even be a general consensus that they "got what they deserved." This often means there is no real public "connect" which results in fewer phone tips, leads and involvement by the public. In many such cases, the victim's own friends and family are reluctant to co-operate with the police and this can severely hamper an investigation.

Conversely, when a "true innocent" is the victim, the public response is often one of genuine fear that this could have happened to them or their loved ones. This motivates them into becoming a valuable asset to police in that they do call in tips and are very willing to co-operate fully, as are the friends and family of the victim. I must also say (and here I am speaking solely from my own experience, but I suspect it may be common to many homicide investigators) that when investigating a case where the victim was a "true innocent," I often felt a personal obligation to be that victim's final advocate; to solve the crime, arrest the suspect and obtain at least a modicum of justice and closure for them and their families — and not just because it was my job.

Issue #2: Ignoring reports

In discussing whether reports of missing women were ignored, we must take a critical look at how missing persons reports are dealt with generally. Firstly, in the vast majority of missing person reports, the person reported as missing is added onto the police computer system and then shows up unharmed. In Canada, 66% of missing persons show up within 24 hours and 85% within one week of the report being filed (Government of Canada 2011). Secondly, in many missing person reports, the disappearance is totally out of character and thus taken more seriously. These missing persons have known addresses, jobs, phone numbers, bank accounts, vehicles and regular contact with family and friends.

Even so, most of these will show up very quickly. If they do not, the police have several avenues of investigation open to them. They can check with known family and friends who are generally happy to co-operate and provide information about the missing person. They can put traces on credit cards, telephone numbers and bank accounts and post vehicle license plates on the system. In some cases, family will generate much public attention via the media, the posting of flyers and even the offering of rewards.

Now take the case of a missing sex trade worker. They are often, by nature, very transient, with many moving from one large center to another without notice. It may well have been several months since they were last in contact with family members. They often have no fixed address, no telephone, no bank account, job or vehicle. Most of their known associates are, for a variety of reasons, reluctant to speak with police, making it difficult to obtain helpful information. While this doesn't mean that the report will be ignored, there are only so many avenues of investigation and only so many resources available to conduct that investigation.

Issue #3: Delay in identifying serial nature

Lastly, we discuss the fact that police took too long to determine the serial nature of the missing women reports and thus failed to apprehend a suspect sooner than they did. Again, were some mistakes made? I'm certain there were, and in fact several high ranking police officers, including the Vancouver police chief, have publicly admitted this.

For the purposes of our discussion, we will look at the challenges this type of case presented to police. I suspect that the main problem with the Pickton investigation is that the *victims were reported as missing and no bodies were recovered.* Think about this for a moment. In the typical serial murder investigation, police start out with a body. That provides irrefutable evidence that a murder has been committed. Then, to offer an exaggerated example, say the body is that of a 22-year-old female who has been strangled with a man's tie and a playing card has been placed on her body. Then, several weeks later, another young female's body is found, strangled with a man's tie and a playing card left on her body.

This would be very clear and overwhelming evidence to support a serial murder investigation. Police would respond quickly and accordingly with the appropriate resources and investigation. In other words, police have bodies, evidence and a basis to begin the appropriate investigation.

Compare this to missing person reports and one begins to see the major differences. With a missing person, particularly those involving people who live below the radar, there is no body and thus, no clear indication that any crime has been committed. In most cases, the missing person reports were made randomly over a substantial length of time.

For example, a missing person report may be made to an officer on A Watch in January, 1996. Another may be made to C Watch in July, 1996, another to D Watch in March, 1997 and so on. Add to that the fact that some reports were even made to totally different police departments. With no bodies and nothing to link the reports together, each report is likely to be recorded onto the police computer without significant follow up. Even if a full investigation were contemplated, we have already identified the problems and challenges when the missing person lives in the criminal world.

LAYING BLAME

Many have accused the police of "failing" these women. Perhaps that's true, but in most cases these women had been failed many times by many different people.

Let's start with the government. Did the government provide adequate services, infrastructure, programs, education and transportation to these victims and their families? Were parents offered the counseling, education and assistance required so that they could provide a supportive and loving home? Were there programs in place to teach them about the importance of encouraging full time attendance at school, assisting with homework and participating in teacher-parent meetings? Was adequate transportation service provided to ensure that these parents and children had easy access to schools, sports, swimming, dance or other extra-curricular activities? Were there even facilities provided for these types of activities?

As they became older, were they encouraged to obtain part time work? Were there even jobs available to them and if so, was the transportation system adequate to make those jobs accessible? Did the parents themselves have the knowledge and abilities required to teach their children the life skills necessary to become successful as an adult and if not, were they offered the opportunity to learn? Were some of these children victimized and vulnerable because they were forced to walk and hitchhike many places due to the lack of adequate and safe transportation? Were these things all available and provided or did the government, and we as a society, fail these families?

How about the education system? Did the schools and teachers ensure these children attended regularly? Did they ensure that curriculum was understood and classes passed successfully or did they simply "move" the student along with little concern about actual learning? Were these children encouraged to seek post-secondary education, trades and vocations? Were resources made available to assist them in doing so? Were incidents of neglect, malnourishment and abuse properly reported to the appropriate social services? Did the schools provide all of this or was there a failure by the education system?

Let's look at social services and child welfare agencies. Were adequate resources allotted to children in need? Were they removed from abusive or neglectful homes? Did they ensure that appropriate schooling and, later on, job training was provided? Did our social services do all that was required or did they too fail these children?

In many cases these victims had early contact with the justice system. Were they treated appropriately or were they simply shunted from one probation officer to another? Did the justice system make any effort to hold parents and family responsible, to ensure appropriate schooling, drug counseling and life skills were part of the process? Or were these victims simply "processed" and ultimately failed by our justice system?

With many of the victims being drug addicted sex trade workers, we must also ask if our government's and thus society's laws, policies and attitudes towards drug use, addiction and prostitution somehow failed these women. Were they forced to live a life in the shadows because of these laws? Were they failed by government policies?

Lastly, we have the police. Did they fail to take the missing women reports seriously enough? Did they marginalize these victims because of who and what they were? I suspect there were individual cases where that did occur. Did they react too slowly in determining a pattern to the disappearances?

Perhaps they did. The simple fact of the matter is that these victims were failed by many different people and agencies for a large portion of their lives. It is simply a fact that very few people go from being healthy, well-adjusted and productive individuals into drug addicted sex trade workers in some magical transformation that occurs overnight. These victims began down the road to drugs and prostitution many years before they in fact became so and the magnitude of the failures were such that no one person, group or agency could have been solely responsible.

Does what we've just discussed excuse mistakes made by police? No, and it's not my intent to excuse those mistakes. As I have repeatedly stated, it is not for me to judge the police. I simply offer the perspective and experience of the police officer, hoping to create a more realistic and educated view for the public to make its judgments.

Many things become clear in hindsight. An apt analogy might be that policing is often like entering a totally dark maze where officers attempt to navigate past obstacles, run into dead ends and feel along walls until they find the light switch. Then, as soon as the lights go on, the media and the public are quick to say, *"How could you miss that? What took so long? Why didn't you do this or that?"* Unfortunately, 'do-overs' based on hindsight are a luxury the police just don't have. Sadly, the media were quick to criticize. Lawyers and family members rapidly joined in. It eventually resulted in an extensive public hearing. Again, there was much finger pointing and after the fact criticism. *Resources that could have been spent on the police were instead spent on second guessing the police.*

Criticism can be used constructively to build or improve, and it can be used destructively, to tear down or destroy. All too often it seems to be the latter. The thing I always wonder is *where were all the critics before the lights went on?*

Police officers know to expect the public scrutiny and arm-chair quarterbacking that almost always occurs in a major police incident or investigation, but that doesn't always make it easier to accept. Most officers truly want and try to do a good job and it can be demoralizing when their best efforts are discredited or de-valued and their motives and even their professionalism questioned.

As the public might expect, there are times when, as a police officer, you rely on training. Sometimes you rely on experience, knowledge or instincts. But sometimes none of that works and it all comes down to luck. Luck, fate, destiny or a higher power, call it what you will. . .but it's nothing *you* control!

CASE STUDY:
Deals with the devil

While stationed on the GIS (Detective) unit in Prince Rupert I became involved in a lengthy homicide investigation. It was a difficult case in that the victim was a known prostitute and drug dealer and at that particular time there were approximately 4,000 transient iron workers living in a work camp just a few miles out of town. Prince Rupert was also the main port for the US Navy, the Canadian Navy and the entire northern fishing fleet. With only four of us working on the file it was overwhelming to say the least.

Early in the investigation I had interviewed Jim Parson and his girlfriend Kathy Dinning. Parson was one of the victim's very few close friends and as such, we felt he might have knowledge about her movements, associates or other matters that might assist our efforts.

Both Parson and Dinning were known to us as small time drug dealers and users. In fact, a few months earlier I'd come across Kathy having a verbal confrontation with an unknown male. She'd been drinking and was in possession of a small amount of marijuana. While she wouldn't say, it was clear she had been roughly treated and was obviously upset. Since the amount was quite small, I decided to simply seize it without charges and gave her a ride home. That one small act of lenience would later save my life.

Jim Parson agreed to cooperate, but it was an uneasy alliance, given that he was a known drug dealer with a criminal past. In one of those "deals with the devil" so common in police work, we agreed that he would provide me with as much information as he could in return for my promise that I wouldn't take any action against him should his information be self-incriminating.

As the investigation progressed, there were several occasions where I attended at Parson's house to clarify a particular point or identify someone the victim may have been seen with. True to his word, he provided information and true to my word, I over-looked anything that was self-incriminating. Sometimes Kathy was there but she hadn't known the victim all that well, so we didn't speak much.

By the time the investigation was about six months old, I had probably been to Parson's house on four or five different occasions. On the last couple visits I noticed that his physical appearance and behavior was deteriorating. He had difficulty focusing and seemed very jumpy and nervous. I simply put it off to his heavy drug use and natural aversion to police and didn't give it much more thought.

On the last and final visit I made to the house I remember waiting quite some time before the door was answered. When it opened, Parson was standing there and I could see Kathy in the background. Jim looked terrible. He had lost weight, his hair was matted and dirty and he was drenched in sweat. Even Kathy looked frightened. I assumed that my arrival had coincided with them having drugs in the house and that the long delay in answering the door was due to them cleaning up and hiding everything. As I only had a few questions to ask, I remained outside while Jim stood in the doorway. After a few moments I had finished with my questions, the conversation ended and I departed.

Two days later we received a call from the RCMP in Vancouver advising us that a female by the name of Kathy Dinning had come to their office with information about a homicide in Prince Rupert. She also said that the only officer she would speak with was me. I immediately flew to Vancouver and set up an interview with her. . .and what she told me still sends a chill up my spine today.

According to Kathy, she had been home alone on the night of the murder. When Jim arrived home it was quite late and she didn't see him, but the next morning he was acting strangely, almost as if in a trance. Later that day, when they heard about the victim's murder, Jim appeared distraught and emotional. She didn't find that strange given that Jim and the victim had been friends for years. In the next few days, things returned to normal. Then I made my first visit to their house.

In her statement, Kathy said that after my initial visit and conversation with Jim, he completely collapsed. He started sweating and was shaking so hard he could barely sit. After several hours she had gotten him calm enough to talk and at that point he confessed the entire murder to her.

He told her how he had gone to the victim for drugs and

she had refused; how he'd gone into a rage and stabbed her to death and that he still couldn't understand how he could have done it. He explained how he had been absolutely certain that I had arrived at his house to arrest him and that he suspected the police were trying to trick him. He was totally shaken and sobbing and when he begged Kathy not to tell anyone she agreed.

As time went on, Jim's behavior and drug use got worse. Kathy stated that every time I arrived at the house he became more and more paranoid and convinced that he was going to be arrested. At the end of each visit he would literally break down and then remain on edge for days. Kathy re-assured him that he could trust me and told him about what I had done for her that night many months past. According to her, Jim remained paranoid and continued to increase his drug use, spiraling downwards to the point that she began to become concerned and even fearful of her own life.

On the day of my final visit to the house Jim was beginning to lose control. His paranoia and heavy drug use was taking its toll and he was acting erratically and unpredictably. When he saw me approaching the house it was the final push and he simply lost it. According to Kathy, he went into his bedroom and when he returned he was carrying a .12 gauge shotgun. When she asked him what he was doing, he told her it was all over and his only hope was to kill me and take off. With that he headed for the door. The same door where I was waiting. . .with no idea of what was about to happen.

What happened was that Kathy Dinning saved my life. She literally placed herself between Parson and the door and begged him to put the gun away. She pleaded and cried and somehow managed to convince him that I was not there to arrest him and that killing me would be a huge mistake. She told him that once

I'd left, they would make plans to leave town and all he needed to do was pull himself together enough for one last conversation with me. She again reminded him of the break I'd given her earlier and how I'd treated her. Whatever she said worked and Jim did put the gun away. When he answered the door, all I saw was the same drugged out, strung out guy I'd been dealing with for months. Little did I know how close I'd come to dying that day.

After I left, Parson deteriorated to the point that his behavior had Kathy frightened that he would kill her or someone else. She spent the remainder of that day almost paralyzed with fear, waited until he was asleep, and then fled to Vancouver. It was only when she felt safe from him that she was prepared to tell her story.

As a result of her information we were able to arrest Parson and execute a search warrant on the house. We recovered the murder weapon and several other pieces of evidence which, in addition to Kathy's statement, was sufficient to convict him of murder and send him to jail for life. And yes. . .we discovered a loaded .12 gauge shotgun in the bedroom.

Amazing! A random act of lenience, the incredible courage of a woman I would not have expected it from, and the element of fate had converged and conspired to save my life, apprehend a killer, and solve a case.

There are no doubt many who may feel that I missed important signs. That my cop instinct must have failed or that I was being careless and inattentive. Perhaps. Certainly there's no question that I didn't suspect Jim Parson of being the murderer, nor did I have any idea about the extreme danger I was in. Should I have? I suppose that fellow on CSI would have!

CASE STUDY:
How could it happen?

During the fall and winter of 1984–85, homes, cabins and trap lines near Teslin Lake in northern British Columbia were being ransacked. Teslin Lake is located on the border of B.C. and the Yukon. The suspect was 40-year-old Michael Oros. Oros was known to be a recluse and a very accomplished outdoorsman, hunter and trapper. He could live for extended periods of time in the bush and could cover an astonishing amount of ground on snowshoes.

Locals who knew him reported that he had been acting even stranger than normal and many were frightened of him. People living in those remote northern areas are very self-sufficient and reluctant to involve outsiders in their business, but the situation had gotten so bad by early 1985 that a complaint was made to the Teslin RCMP. Given the nature of the suspect and the terrain, it was determined that the matter might have to be dealt with using a trained Emergency Response Team (ERT). Thus, responsibility for the arrest was turned over to the ERT team in Prince Rupert, 680 miles away.

It must be understood that the area Oros was travelling through was vast and covered by dense stands of trees and bush. Some of the cabins and trap lines he had pilfered were over 100 miles away from the nearest village and reachable only by snow-shoe or snowmobile. One of the major challenges was to pinpoint his location sufficiently so that a patrol could be sent out and have some reasonable chance of locating him. The Teslin Lake locals agreed to report any sightings or new break-ins and the ERT team made plans for an immediate departure should they receive that information.

On March 18, 1985, a resident of Whitehorse, Yukon, checked his cabin and found that it had been ransacked and much of its contents stolen. He observed Michael Oros fleeing across the frozen lake with the stolen goods and called the Teslin RCMP. They immediately chartered an aircraft and flew over the area. Spotting Oros crossing a frozen lake, they made a low pass to confirm his identity, and were shot at by the suspect. The search plane broke off its surveillance; and the Emergency Response Teams in Prince Rupert was notified.

I was stationed in Prince Rupert at the time. While I wasn't a member of the ERT and had not yet taken the hostage negotiator course, I had worked with them several times due to the fact that there was no trained negotiator available. I was personal friends with almost everyone on the team and had immense respect for every one of them. In fact, about two weeks prior to the March 18 sighting of Oros, I'd had a house party and two of the atten-dees were team members Constable Mike Buday and Constable Garry Rodgers.

Buday was the team's dog handler and he and Garry Rodgers were best friends. Friends — but quite different from each other. Garry was a slender, quiet man and an extremely gifted investigator. Mike was simply larger than life. He was a big man who possessed incredible physical strength. He was boisterous, funny and the life of any party. He was one of those people who smiled with his whole face. My last memory of Mike Buday and that huge smile was of him standing on my old beat up coffee table telling some joke. I never saw him alive again.

On March 19, the Prince Rupert ERT team arrived via plane at Teslin Lake. Oros had camped in the bush overnight and in the morning hours of March 19, moved onto the open lake surface. He was spotted heading for the densely treed shoreline and the ERT team determined that they could land and set up in such a manner that they could intercept him while he was still in the open and before he had a chance to reach the bush. But Oros was moving much more quickly than anyone had thought possible.

The team was able to deploy but Oros had covered so much ground so quickly that he was able to enter the bush sooner than anticipated and approximately 400 yards away from where the team had deployed. At this point Oros's knowledge and experience in the bush put him at an extreme advantage. Moving almost silently, he was able to circle in behind and downwind of Cst. Buday, his police dog Trooper and the others who were strung out in a perimeter. From a position of ambush and without warning, Oros fired his rifle, striking Cst. Buday in the head and killing him instantly. Cst. Rodgers, alerted by the shot, turned and observed Oros approximately 50 yards away with his rifle pointed directly at him. Rodgers fired a single, instinctual shot from his M16 rifle. Oros was struck in the forehead and died instantly.

34

In reconstructing the scene, investigators were amazed to discover that Cst. Rodgers shot had been nothing short of miraculous. Based on the suspect's height and his location relative to tree limbs, branches and bush, Rodgers' instinctive shot, from 50 yards away, had hit a target approximately 3" square! It also became clear that had Oros not been killed, he would very likely have been able to circle around and literally pick off each individual team member from behind.

During the subsequent investigation, Oros' weapon was seized and examined by firearms experts at the RCMP crime lab. What they discovered is literally inexplicable. The shell that was removed from Oros' rifle had a firing pin mark on it. This meant that Oros had in fact pulled the trigger while aiming at Rodgers, but the shell had not fired. *Additional tests could find nothing wrong with either the rifle or that particular shell.*

Ten years after the incident, renowned Native artist Roy Henry Vickers, decided to create a painting as a tribute to Cst. Mike Buday. Garry Rodgers accompanied him back to Teslin Lake. In spite of passing time, he was able to walk directly and unerringly to the murder site.

Upon arriving, he was quoted as saying, "I'm shaking again. It was two years after Mike's death before I could talk about it without breaking out in a sweat and starting to shake, and here I am shaking again." He went on to say, "You can call it a higher spirit, God, whatever you want, but it's hard to argue with that physical evidence. It was as if my bullet that day was guided."

Garry and the rest of the ERT team went on to have successful and honorable careers. Years later it was my great honor to once again work with the officer who had been the team leader that fateful day. We never really talked about it much. We remembered and honored Mike. But the pain of what had happened and what he'd seen that day was evident in his eyes. He hadn't been injured that day, but neither had he escaped unscathed. None of us did. We'd lost a friend and come face to face with our own mortality.

I wondered if it had been worth the cost, for a few old cabins damaged and some belongings stolen. But I know that is *not* what Mike Buday died to protect. He died protecting the law. He died protecting his colleagues and fellow citizens. And he died doing what he strongly believed in — what every police officer should believe in...his duty.

Were there people who felt that this should not have happened? That the police should have been better trained...more prepared? Did some wonder how a single suspect could out-maneuver a team of trained police officers? I'm sure there were. I'm also sure that they'd have felt and thought differently if they had been there. If they'd seen and experienced the conditions. Or if they had known the quality and abilities of those officers. I wonder if they would have put their own lives on the line like Mike Buday did?

———

Yes, as a society, we have high expectations of our police officers, and frankly we should. Furthermore, most officers and police actions live up to or even exceed those expectations. But we ask much of these young men and women. Do we base our expectations on perceptions and ideals that are unrealistic except in some movie script? Do we set the bar too high?

How is it that a single mistake made by a single or very small number of officers can ignite an entire city to riot? Cause the media and the public to go into a frenzy, and literally taint an entire police department and every officer in it with one broad brush stroke? (as in the case of Amadou Diallo or Rodney King)?

———

Should we be completely shocked when individual officers fail, when they use poor judgment, when they use excessive force, when they show fear in the face of danger, anger in the face of abuse or when they are affected and succumb to the constant exposure to society's darker side? In short, when they fail to live up to the public's perhaps unrealistic expectations?

3

THE JUDGMENT FACTOR

To judge that of which you know naught is truly an
arrogant endeavor and speaks more to the character
of those who judge than those being judged!

Police officers and police actions are often subject to intense
scrutiny, differing opinions and, in many cases, a rush to judgment. . .and it's almost always after the fact. Because the general
public is interested in policing and because their perceptions
and expectations of policing are often skewed, many judgments
are also skewed. More often than not, the public or the media
don't have the *whole* story and are unaware of the mitigating
circumstances.

In actual fact, it's pretty easy to find positive and negative
incidents involving any and every police force. Sometimes officers will simply make the wrong decision, lose their temper and
control or lack the skills or personality to adequately handle a
particular situation. This should not be terribly surprising. The
very nature of police work places officers into conflict situations
involving violent and emotional situations where they are often
subject to physical and verbal abuse and are required to make
almost impossible decisions under the worst of conditions. . .and
time and time again they do so with amazing success.

But, like any human endeavor, there is the human error factor. Most humans will go their entire adult lives and never be

involved in a serious physical or even verbal confrontation. Police officers are involved in just such incidents day after day; week after week; month after month; year after year. Officers are routinely cursed at, assaulted, have their families threatened, are spit upon, have feces thrown at them or deal with any number of other extremely challenging situations. They may have acquitted themselves well on most occasions, over long periods of time. But simple common sense and the law of averages should tell us that when you take humans, with the inevitable human error factor and insert them into volatile, emotional and violent situations over and over, time after time, that eventually something will go wrong.

Imagine then that one shift an officer comes to work distracted by personal issues. It could be an argument with a spouse, lack of sleep because of a sick child, money or health worries or any of the myriad of issues that can occur with any human being. This time, when the drunk spits on them or threatens their family or the suspect resists or becomes abusive, they fail the test. They snap and treat the suspect roughly. The action is caught on tape and the world will judge that officer's entire career on a five second videotape. It simply will not matter that they have dealt with hundreds of similar situations with restraint, self control and professionalism.

Ironically, the ones who will be quickest to judge are those who have likely never even been tested let alone passed the test. It's like the soldier who fights bravely in 19 fire fights and on the twentieth breaks down and runs. Those who will sit in judgment may well never have been in a single fire fight...and yet they will judge. And that soldier's career, integrity and courage will be measured based solely on that twentieth fight.

CASE STUDY:
Breaking point

For reasons that will become apparent, I have chosen to keep the names and locations of the police officer and the police department anonymous. There is simply nothing to be gained by adding to the already extensive grief this officer's family has already undergone.

In 2008, a police officer working in a smaller suburban area, located just outside a large mid western US city, was videotaped assaulting a handcuffed suspect. It was violent and drew massive criticism from the media and the public. There were numerous demands that he be fired immediately, that he be arrested, held without bail and sent to prison. The officer was portrayed as brutal and corrupt and both he and his family were subject to extensive abuse, including death threats. The officer was charged, media interest dwindled and that was the information and image with which the public was left.

The *whole* story follows: This officer had a stellar and distinguished career spanning 15 years. He was active and well liked in his community where he coached sports, was a member of a service club and attended his local church. Approximately four weeks prior to the incident, this officer's 16-year-old daughter had been assaulted and raped while walking in a nearby park. The officer and his family were devastated. His wife suffered a break down and his daughter started intensive counseling. As the husband, father and protector, the officer felt he had failed. He confessed to a counselor that he was angry, helpless and frustrated, couldn't sleep and yet felt that he had to appear strong for his family.

The case went unsolved. Four weeks later another young girl was assaulted and raped near the same park. A suspect fled on foot but was finally cornered and arrested. This suspect appeared to be high on drugs, was aggressive and abusive. While being arrested, he mocked the police by bragging that he'd done it before and not been caught. The officer lost control of his emotions and assaulted the suspect. It was this assault that was captured on video and broadcast to the public. The suspect's DNA subsequently linked him to the earlier rape of the officer's daughter.

Now you have the *complete* story. Did the officer fail, use bad judgment and commit an offence? Yes he did. Should he be held accountable? Yes he should be. What should be done with him? Should he be fired? Should he go to jail? If so, for how long? Could or would you have done better? You be the judge...the public and the media have already taken their turn.

CASE STUDY:
The harshest critic

In 2009, police in a large city in the eastern US received a call of shots being fired in or near an abandoned building in one of the cities high crime areas. This was a fairly typical call for the area and several patrol officers were dispatched. The following account is based on statements made by the attending officers and evidence gathered during the subsequent internal investigation.

Upon arriving the officers observed a vacant four story building. It was dark and most of the windows had been boarded over. As they approached and entered the building, they drew their weapons and loudly identified themselves, but received no response. There was no electricity and the officer's only light came from their flashlights.

While clearing the main floor, the officers could hear the sound of movement on one of the upper floors. They again identified themselves, ordering anyone inside to reveal themselves. Still there was no response. They ascended the stairs slowly, and at the top, observed a foyer like area which had several doors leading to separate rooms or offices.

As they began to clear the second floor, 25-year-old patrol officer Ronald Grey and 32-year-old patrol officer Greg Rivera opened one of the doors and identified themselves as police officers. Officer Rivera checked to the right and Grey the left. Almost immediately a closet door to the left was flung open and someone stepped out. Both officers instinctively turned and a flashlight beam glinted off of an object in the person's hand. Officer Grey fired.

The victim turned out to be a 13-year-old African American boy who had been playing in the abandoned building. According to his friends, they all did so quite often. The object he had been holding turned out to be a plastic toy pistol the boy had been playing with. A tragedy on every level.

The public and media went into a frenzy. Because the officer was Caucasian, there were accusations of racism and demands that he be charged with murder. The police department was accused of protecting him and covering up. The criticism was relentless. . .the facts ignored.

In the end, it was not the public's criticism and judgment which turned out to be the harshest. Seven days after the shooting, Officer Ronald Grey was found dead in his home. His death was determined to be a suicide.

CASE STUDY:
Too much to bear

In October 2008, New York City police received a call about a dangerous, emotionally disturbed male acting in an erratic manner. The call was assigned to the elite Emergency Services Unit and the officer in charge was veteran Lt. Michael Pigott.

Lt. Pigott arrived on the scene and observed naked 35-year-old former mental patient, Iman Morales, acting very erratically. He was perched on a 10-foot-high wall and swinging a long electrical light fixture at anyone who came close. He was unable or unwilling to engage the officers in conversation and showed no sign of surrendering. After some time had expired, Lt. Pigott gave the order for one of his officers to deploy a Taser. The suspect was hit, fell from the wall and subsequently died. The very thing that Pigott had hoped to avoid had occurred and he immediately took full responsibility for the incident. As per departmental policy for police involved deaths, Lt. Pigott was placed on administrative suspension pending an investigation.

The media went to work and they had a heyday. They reported that Lt. Pigott had been responsible for the suspect's death and that it had not been justified. They reported that he had been suspended and had his badge and firearm "stripped" from him. There were numerous calls by community activists, the suspect's family members and the media for Pigott to be indicted for murder. From many accounts, Pigott himself felt responsible for the suspect's death and spent considerable time replaying the events and wondering if he should have or could have done something differently. He also felt betrayed and unsupported by his department's lack of response to public and media comments, and felt that his 21 years of excellent service counted for nothing. He told his wife, "My life is on the line. My job is on the line."

According to the many officers who knew and had worked with him, Lt. Pigott was an excellent police officer whose 21-year career had been filled with many difficult and dangerous situations. He had faced them all with courage and honor, earning respect and achieving many unqualified successes. He was described as a wonderful husband, father, son and friend. But he found himself ill prepared for the barrage leveled at him by the media. Their fire was relentless and merciless.

Eight days later, Lt. Michael Pigott drove to his station and wrote an apology letter to his wife in which he told her "I'm sorry for the mess, I was just trying to protect my guys that day. I can't bear to lose my family and go to jail." He then clipped the lock off a fellow officer's locker, removed a nine millimeter pistol, and took his own life.

This tragedy left two people dead. Two families damaged. Lt. Pigott left behind a wife and three children. A dedicated and honorable police officer who made one questionable decision in a career spanning over 20 years. An imperfect decision in an imperfect world.

I wonder. Had Lt. Pigott survived the onslaught of negative press coverage and the rush to judgment, might he have warned all officers to prepare emotionally for that imperfect world? Would he have warned them that the aftermath can be as deadly to officers as the calls themselves?

Hopefully Lt. Pigott has now found a perfect world and a level of forgiveness and understanding that he could not find in this one.

Shortly after his death, the victim's family sued Lt. Pigott's estate.

Yes, we do expect much. But how do we ask the things we do of our police officers and fellow human beings and then so quickly turn on them when they need our support, our compassion, our understanding? Why the rush to judgment?

Many experts believe that one of the reasons is that the public simply are unaware of the limitations, the physics and the realities of physical confrontations.

PUBLIC EDUCATION

In 2010, in response to several police shootings, the Oregon legislature mandated that each county devise a standardized and transparent system for handling police involved shootings. Included was a directive that there be some component of public education about the realities and the myths surrounding law enforcement's use of deadly force.

One of the first to respond with a protocol was District Attorney Alex Gardner of Lane County. To fulfill the public education requirement, the county initially launched a series of day-long exercises that involved exposing local reporters and politicians to shoot/don't shoot scenario training. They found this to be expensive and difficult to manage. They also found that the turnover of reporters was high and thus the benefits of the training were short lived.

In 2011, the county decided to produce an online video that would always be available for public access as well as for use as an explanation or to counter the kind of misinformation that seems to commonly arise after any police-involved shooting. They felt that this would allow basic facts about deadly force to be communicated even when officials couldn't comment publicly on the specifics of an ongoing investigation.

Dr. Bill Lewinski Ph.D., executive director of the Force Science Institute, agreed to appear on camera to deliver pertinent findings emerging from FSI research. Dr. Alexis Artwohl, Ph.D., a Force Science board advisor and certification course faculty member known for her work in police behavioral science, joined in the video production. The project was filmed and edited by a professional production company.

Lewinski and Artwohl's goal was to first determine which primary questions, concerns and accusations arose in the aftermath of most police involved shootings and then provide general answers and information that might offer logical and factual explanations and dispel some of the myths held by the public and media. A condensed version of the video is as follows:

Hollywood Brainwashing

In the opening minutes, Artwohl points out three ironies about the public perception of police involved major incidents:

1. Civilians commonly expect events to defy the laws of physics.

2. Officers are expected to defy the limits of human performance by having perfect memories and perfect decision-making, when research clearly shows that to be impossible.

3. The judging of police officers and police actions are often based on myths, assumptions, and personal opinions that may not necessarily be true.

District Attorney Gardner then suggests that these critical misconceptions stem in large part from brainwashing of the public mind by Hollywood. He states, "Our video culture conveys a tremendous amount of misinformation about police operations and behaviour." He goes on to say, "The extent to which the public relies on what they see on TV and in the movies, often without even being fully aware of it, makes it very difficult for people to evaluate whether an officer has behaved appropriately in a use-of-force application."

Busting Myths

The bulk of the video then focuses on myths about police-involved shootings, phrased in the form of naive but potentially inflammatory questions that DA Gardner says frequently arise from the media and community activists after offenders are shot by police.

Here's an abridged sampling. In some cases, the online video includes real-life vehicle dashboard camera (dash-cam) footage to help illustrate the problems discussed.

"Why didn't the police talk the aggressor down?"

Dr. Artwohl points out that most of the time, officers do talk people down, using their communication and persuasion skills. Research shows that only about one percent of all calls for service result in any use of force, and only a very small percentage of those result in use of deadly force.

She states, "Not all offenders can be talked out of what they're getting ready to do. At that point, the only thing an officer can do is use force to protect his life and protect the public."

Lewinski mentions that sometimes because of chemical, mental, emotional, or other issues, subjects are unable to listen to anything, and then adds, "That means they are in control of the situation. The officer is the reactor and has to respond to what the person is doing. It's not the officer's choice, usually, to avoid using verbal skills. It's the person being unable to listen or attend or being unwilling to do what the officer is saying."

"It was just a knife and the officer had a gun. Why didn't the officer just disarm the subject?"

"Some people think an individual armed with a knife is not a dangerous threat to an officer," Lewinski says. "From our research and the research of others, we know that not to be true. Knives can actually be more dangerous than a gun."

Dr. Lewinski explains that force science studies show that a young person in reasonably good shape can cover as much as 31 feet in the time it takes an officer to draw his gun, point, and fire one round. If a person is seven feet away, the officer could even have his gun in the low-ready position, and by the time he raises the gun and fires even once, he could be stabbed. He says, "A stab from a knife or a stab and upward cut can be extremely quick. Each cut or slash can occur in less than one-quarter second, and any one could be lethal for the officer...."

"Why not shoot the gun or knife out of their hand? Why not shoot to wound the subject?"

Lewinski recalls TV and movies in which the hero defeats an attacker with this kind of precision shooting. "It's one of those Hollywood myths," he says. "It looks good on film but doesn't work in the real world. Officers do not have the ability to fire and hit that accurately in a dynamic encounter."

Even if officers aim for center mass, they "tend not to be as accurate as they might be on the range because the dynamics by which people move in a real-world encounter are such that center mass is a constantly changing target...."

Dr. Lewinski states that the goal of police use of deadly force is to stop the threat, and that the best place an officer can aim for is center mass. He explains. "Even then it's not a guarantee," but it's more realistic than the extraordinary challenge of intentionally hitting only an arm or a leg.

"Why were they shot in the back?"

In framing an answer to this nettlesome question, Dr. Lewinski describes a shooting in which he served as an expert witness. When the officer made the decision to shoot, the threatening suspect was facing him full-on. Yet when the smoke cleared, the officer's rounds were found to have struck in the suspect's side and back, making it appear that the officer had not been in jeopardy when he fired.

Lewinski says that in a life threatening situation, an officer will generally fire four rounds per second, discharging a bullet every quarter-second. In that eye-blink, the suspect had begun to turn away and fall through the pattern of shots, a movement the officer would not have had time to detect and react to. Inevitably, the subject's side and back were exposed in the process to the line of fire. "Very true, shots did go into the back," Lewinski says. But in the time span involved, "there was nothing the officer could have done to stop from shooting the subject in the back."

In the video, Lewinski demonstrates the twisting-and-turning movement involved.

"Doesn't a video of an event tell the whole story?"

Dr. Lewinski responds, "In a word, No." A video camera, Lewinski explains, records action from one particular perspective, and that's very limiting in its ability to tell the full story. "Look at the number of cameras necessary for referees to look at during a football game in attempting to accurately and completely judge an action under scrutiny," he says.

In a video recording, which people tend to think is an accurate reporter of any particular incident, some action may be missing entirely, and what's shown can be significantly skewed. Lewinski references a camera some officers now wear that sits just in front of an officer's ear.

"This reportedly has the view of the officer, but it does not. If you close your left eye, for instance, you will see what your right eye sees. Your right eye sees a different field of view than your left eye. Now imagine a camera far behind your right eye. What does that see? No camera records things as an officer's eyes and brain record it."

Officer Involved Shooting Procedures

After the myth-busting segments, which also include reaction-time realities and less-lethal devices, the video concentrates on a walk-through of investigative procedures, given by DA Gardner. Among other things, they explain how the deadly force investigative team operates and why investigations sometimes take months to complete.

Gardner expresses empathy with the public and media being frustrated because a lot of information isn't released immediately. He says, "It's frustrating for the police, too. We want to get the story out, especially when an officer has done something heroic. But we need to wait so as not to taint the investigation."

Artwohl notes in conclusion, "Most officers will tell you that by far the most stressful part of the event is what happens afterwards. We need to refrain from a rush to judgment. The least we can do is to provide officers the benefit of the doubt while the investigation is going on."

IN CONCLUSION

Public feedback on the video has been "very positive," Gardner says, "but where we'll get the most is on the heels of the next shooting." Meanwhile, he encourages other policing agencies to benefit from the production, which Gardner describes as "a lasting tool to help educate people who are unfamiliar with law enforcement use of deadly force and how it is investigated. Officers deserve that community understanding. They've earned it."

Artwohl agrees. "The video, with its expert observations, can be accessible for years to come, whenever questions come up about shootings," she says. "At times when an agency might be unable to comment directly on a lethal force event, the video can speak for the agency about controversial or misunderstood issues." The concept of having such a video or DVD available is one that every department should consider. Any information or tool that educates the public about the actions, limitations and abilities of the police may well reduce the negative impact of incidents that are so often misunderstood and wrongly judged.

In so many cases, education and information is the light that illuminates knowledge and understanding.

Perhaps it's fitting to end the chapter with this thought: Wise, thoughtful men will use hindsight as a tool for improvement and learning. Small minded, petty men will use hindsight as a tool for judgement and criticism.

4

THE UNEXPECTED OUTCOME

The result of an action often blinds us to its intent.

The very nature of police work places officers in confrontational situations where the outcome can vary greatly depending upon the decisions and actions of the individual officer and on the decisions or actions of the person(s) they are interacting with. In any tactical situation and many others, the consequences of an officer's decision or action can be incredibly serious and are often judged not on the circumstances but on the outcome.

The real problem is that human beings make decisions and take action based on so many different factors that it would be literally impossible to predict. For example, just a few basic factors might include alcohol, drugs, mental health, emotional stability, gender, physical abilities, familiarity with weapons, history with police, or motivation. Of course, many times it's a combination of several factors.

This means that an officer cannot rely solely on experience, science, formula, patterns or studies, and must try to make decisions based on all of the data and information they can gather regarding the current incident. Then they have to make their best guess as to what the suspect might do or how they might react.

Many refer to this as the "gut instinct" that officers can develop over time and with experience. As you might imagine, gut instinct is not a science and sometimes fails. Sometimes the outcome of a situation is much more dependent on the decisions or actions of someone or something that is totally beyond the control of the police. Sometimes you're damned if you do and damned if you don't.

CASE STUDY:
Hostage crisis

In Surrey, B.C., police received a call about a male suspect who had taken his girlfriend and sister hostage and was currently barricaded in his house. As the hostage negotiator, my role was to work in conjunction with the Emergency Response Team and the incident commander, set up a communications link with the suspect and engage him in conversation. The ultimate goal of course, was securing the safe release of the hostages and the safe arrest of the suspect.

We had very little useful information about the suspect, but based on hours of training, years of personal experience and the collective experience of many similar situations throughout the world, we knew that the longer we could engage the suspect and keep him talking, the greater our chances for a safe and success-ful outcome.

Initially, things went according to plan. I made contact with him and began a conversation. He appeared to be sober and while very stressed, had the ability to speak logically and clearly. After several hours he agreed to release his sister and we were able to get her out of the house safely. From information we obtained from her, we knew that he was in fact armed with a rifle, that he was stressed and agitated but had not actually harmed any-one. Based on that, I strongly recommended to the incident commander that we continue with negotiations and hold off on any forced entry. A short while later I heard the shot that still haunts me to this day.

A young girl was dead and I will forever wonder if we could have or should have done something different. In spite of overwhelming data to the contrary, time and talk did not save her. I will never forget her father's agony. I will never forget that tragedy. I will live the rest of my life wondering what went wrong.

CASE STUDY:
To fire or not to fire

In 1978, I was a young, inexperienced officer working in the relatively quiet town of Parksville on Vancouver Island. One day we received a call of a domestic dispute at a home located on an acreage in a rural part of the district. It was during the day shift so the corporal suggested that he and I attend. While on route he explained that the house we were going to was owned by a male subject who was known to be "anti-police" and who'd had violent interactions with the police before. We had no information about his access to firearms.

As we arrived, both of us were very alert and aware of the potential for danger. We parked towards the end of the long driveway and began to approach the house, which was in actual fact a mobile trailer. As we got closer, I could hear loud yelling and screaming from inside, but it sounded more angry than fearful. I couldn't see any movement inside but noted that there was a vehicle parked approximately 15 feet from the trailer and there was a small raised porch leading to the front door. My partner was leading and I was trailing about 10 feet behind. When he got to within five or six feet of the front door, it flew open, and out emerged a very agitated male pointing a large bore rifle directly at my partner's chest.

I remember that time seemed to slow and my focus narrowed totally and completely on that male and that gun. I was immediately beside the parked vehicle and was able to take cover behind it, draw my weapon and take direct aim at the male. Thus began one of the most agonizing decisions I would ever have to make in my career. . .to fire or not to fire?

I can still clearly remember the thought process, occurring in literally milliseconds. I knew that I was qualified as an expert marksman and would not miss from that distance. I knew that it was highly unlikely that a .38 caliber round would be instantly fatal. I knew that even a reactive shot fired by the suspect would be unlikely to miss from that close range. I knew that almost any shot from a large rifle was likely to be fatal to my partner. I knew that in the time it had taken me to get behind cover, draw and aim my weapon, the suspect had plenty of time to fire if that was his intention. And I knew that no matter what decision I made, if it was the wrong one, it would result in my partner's death. I did not fire.

I have no idea how, but my partner was able to remain calm and started to talk with the suspect. After a few minutes he began to settle down and had even lowered the rifle so that it was no longer pointed directly at anyone. Just as I was beginning to feel that the critical moment had passed, that the suspect had calmed to the point that we could safely withdraw, the trailer door flew open again and this time it was the suspect's wife armed with a shotgun.

So the entire process began again. With her appearance, the male suspect became agitated and threatening again. We now had two armed suspects, both pointing weapons at my partner. Certain that my previous decision had now signed his death warrant, I could only hold steady, knowing that the situation had deteriorated to the point that nothing I did now could prevent my partner being shot. That any offensive action on my part would surely end badly. Again, I did not fire.

By some miracle the suspects didn't fire either and we were able to retreat, call for assistance and secure the scene. Many hours later, negotiators were able to secure their surrender without a shot being fired or a single injury occurring.

As for me? Well, it was several hours before I had stopped shaking enough to actually write a report. And I'm pretty certain my corporal went home and hugged his wife and kids. The courage he displayed that day was incredible. It didn't win him any medals or awards. No parades, accolades or fortune. But it did earn him my lifelong respect and admiration.

This was just one potentially lethal situation during my career where the outcome was determined in part by the decisions and actions of the police officers and in part by the decisions and actions of the suspects. I've often wondered what would have happened had the suspect shot my partner. Would I have been criticized for not firing? Would the media or the public have accused me of failing in my responsibilities? I don't really know.

What I do know is that I would have had to face his wife and children and wonder if my actions had cost them a husband and father. I would have had to face my fellow officers and wonder if my actions had cost them a friend and colleague. And I know I would have had to face myself and ask those same questions every day for the rest of my life.

Such is the fine line many police officers tread where fate, luck or the decisions of others can play such an important part in the outcome. There is a possibility that no matter what you do, things can go badly. Because sometimes, when chance knocks, fate answers.

CASE STUDY:
Taser death of Robert Dziekanski

In 2007, police working at Vancouver's International Airport received a report of a man acting erratically in the airport arrivals area. They attended the scene and what happened next became one of the most controversial police actions in Canadian history.

When the four RCMP officers arrived they had almost no information other than the fact that there was a male, later identified as Robert Dziekanski, acting erratically and aggressively. They found him in a secure arrivals area, a large room surrounded by large glass windows and containing a few pieces of office furniture, which he had been throwing around. He was visibly agitated and the officers were unable to verbally communicate with him. He was holding an office stapler, pacing around, waving his arms and speaking in a language unfamiliar to any of the officers. Rightly or wrongly, the decision was quickly made to deploy a Taser. It's difficult to know for certain what led to this decision, but I will discuss it in more detail later in the chapter.

It's important to remember that the Taser was a Force-sanctioned weapon and these officers had been trained to believe that it was a safe and effective method of taking control of a *violent* or *resisting* suspect. In any event, one of the officers deployed the

Taser and while there is some dispute about whether it malfunctioned or whether it was deployed incorrectly, there is no dispute that Mr. Dziekanski was hit five times and subsequently went into cardiac arrest and died.

The incident was captured on an amateur video and showed very little time had elapsed from the officer's arrival to the deployment of the Taser. It also appeared that the officers were more focused on securing the suspect in handcuffs than making efforts to resuscitate him. Without question, the optics of the situation were not good.

It was later discovered that Mr. Dziekanski had arrived in Vancouver on an international flight from Poland, that he spoke no English, suffered from some mental health issues and that he was to be met at the arrivals area by his mother. Mr. Dziekanski became disoriented and it is estimated that he spent between 10 and 12 hours wandering around the customs and baggage claim areas unchallenged or unassisted by any customs or airport personnel in spite of the fact that his mother had made several requests for help.

Eventually she left the airport and returned home. By the time the police became involved, Mr. Dziekanski was hungry, dehydrated and clearly stressed. As so often happens, the police inherited a problem caused by the failures or actions of others.

So let's examine what happened, how decisions may have been made, the factors that may have influenced those decisions and how the outcome was so very different from what the officers expected.

Firstly, it must be understood that when several officers are involved in a tactical situation it is normal and generally advisable for the most senior or experienced officer to take charge. These types of incidents can require split second decisions and immediate action and simply do not lend themselves to committee or group discussions and input.

While some may be critical of this approach and accuse junior officers of "blindly" following orders, consider for a moment a situation where a junior officer does not follow an order or obey a command and a member of the public or a co-worker is killed as a result. It is just not acceptable in a tactical incident. Conversely, tactical commanders or senior officers on the scene must be prepared to take responsibility for their decisions and for the commands or orders they may have given. They must be accountable to their own superiors and to the public, and in my opinion, make clear that the actions taken by junior officers were done so at their command and direction.

Now let's dissect the situation to see how the senior officer may have processed the available data and information he did have. For this purpose I will discuss the data or information the officer had or could assume and the thought process or how he analyzed that data.

Data:
The suspect was a male located in a secured arrivals area of a large airport.

Analysis:
He had to have gone through security as well as Canada Customs and has not accessed the public areas.

Data:
He is acting in an irrational and erratic manner, pacing and waving his arms. He is holding an office stapler or similar item and he does not calm down when uniformed police arrive on the scene.

Analysis:

It could mean substance abuse, mental health issues or anger and frustration with something or someone. Almost every logically and rationally thinking adult in the world knows that a person in uniform represents authority and will calm down if they wish to resolve whatever issue or problem they are having. Since the suspect had not had any contact with police prior to this and therefore had no reason to be angry or frustrated with them, it could be assumed his problem is not simple anger or frustration. The logical assumption then is that the problem is substance abuse or mental health. Furthermore, as the suspect had just gone through Security and Customs it was possible but unlikely that he was under influence of an illicit substance so odds are high it is a mental or emotional problem.

Data:

The senior officer knows that he must take the suspect into custody for his own and for the public safety and that the options available to do this are:

1. to verbally engage the suspect in an effort to calm him to the point that he will voluntarily accompany the officers;

2. to physically engage the suspect with overwhelming force;

3. to deploy pepper spray in an effort to bring him under control, or

4. to deploy a Taser in an effort to bring him under control.

Analysis:

- That no verbal solution was available due to language, emotional or mental health issues.

- That an attempt to overpower the suspect would risk injury to the suspect and that in the case of the officers, being struck in the face by even a small item like an office stapler could result in the loss of an eye.

- Use of pepper spray in the confined area would affect the officers as well as the suspect and could well cause the suspect to become more enraged, especially if he was suffering from a mental health or substance abuse issue.

- The Taser is a department sanctioned, non-lethal weapon designed to incapacitate a suspect without causing injury to the suspect, the officers or the public and that deploying it would be the best option.

At this point it is unclear exactly what occurred. According to the officer who deployed the Taser, it did not operate correctly and Mr. Dziekanski remained standing. The officer continued to deploy the Taser until finally the suspect fell to the ground and was handcuffed. Tragically, Mr. Dziekanski died at the scene. Autopsy results revealed that he had been hit a total of five times with the Taser and had died from heart failure.

There was massive public outrage. The officers were accused of everything from negligence to murder. It reached such a point that it caused a significant international incident and resulted in a lengthy and comprehensive public inquiry.

At the end of the inquiry several issues remained unclear, one being whether the Taser itself had caused death or whether the officer had deployed it improperly. Much evidence was given by both sides of the debate as to the safety of Tasers. In spite of the fact that there was really no conclusive proof that Tasers themselves caused death or serious injury, it was decided that the police should be strictly limited in their ability to use them. The result was a national moratorium and policy change on police use of Tasers.

Now imagine if things had worked the way these officers *expected* they would be, based on their training and experience. The suspect would have collapsed to the ground unharmed and the officers would have placed him in restraints, taken him to cells and the entire matter would have been a non-issue, just like hundreds of similar situations every day.

In this case, however, the suspect suffered a heart attack and the *outcome* of the officer's decision was far different than what they wanted or expected. It's important to repeat that. *None of those officers wanted or expected Mr. Dziekanski to die!* It was a tragic outcome and they were judged on that outcome rather than on the decisions and actions they took based on the information available to them.

ALTERNATE SCENARIOS

To further illustrate the point, allow me to expand further with a different scenario. Suppose, instead of a Taser, the officers had decided they would try to physically restrain the suspect? What if, in the altercation, the suspect fell, struck his head on the desk and died? Or an officer was struck with the stapler and lost an eye? I suspect many would have been critical, stating that they were issued Tasers for a reason and had failed to use the best possible method available to them. Again, judgment based on the outcome and not the action.

Lastly, suppose they had decided to simply try talking to and calming the subject down. What if, in spite of that, he became so agitated that he threw a chair through the plate glass window and a section of it struck and killed a civilian on the other side? Or if he had ran and jumped through the window himself? Without doubt, many would accuse the officers of not acting quickly enough.

As is always the case whenever any level of force is employed by the police, every single option available to the officers had the potential of an unexpected and disastrous outcome.

These are just a few sample scenarios of one situation which illustrate how an outcome can vary dramatically depending on myriad factors beyond the predictability of the officer. It demonstrates how the unexpected, fate and even luck can play a part in the outcome of a situation, especially one involving use of force.

It must be stated that in the above example, the senior officer on the scene (the one presumably making the decisions) had significant personal and substance abuse issues himself. His subsequent actions in an unrelated matter clearly proved that he was a problem or *rogue* officer and in the face of dismissal from the force, he elected to resign.

At this point I'm not sure anyone can really tell whether this officer's personality and problems influenced the actions of the subordinate officers, but one could certainly understand how that would be possible. If these junior officers were in fact following the lead and commands of this senior officer, how culpable are they?

Most of the media and many in the public continued to call for the officers to be arrested and charged. It eventually culminated with each of the officers being charged with perjury as a result of testimony they gave in the inquiry. The case is still before the courts five years later.

Because those charges are pending at publication time, I will make no further comment other than to say that if in fact they did deliberately lie under oath, then each individual officer must stand responsible and should be dealt with harshly. When determining this, it may be helpful to consider the effects of Combat Stress Amnesia as discussed in the Chapter Six: Combat Stress Syndrome.*

CASE STUDY:
Innocent bystander

In 2010, a Florida Sheriff's Department received a call of a male acting erratically in a local downtown restaurant. Two sheriff's deputies attended and on arrival noted a small crowd of bystanders on the sidewalk in front of the establishment. The deputies made their way inside and observed several tables of customers eating and being served by staff.

The restaurant owner and two staff members were engaged in trying to calm a male customer who appeared to be under the influence of alcohol or drugs or who was suffering from mental

---

* On July 29, 2013 the first of these four officers was acquitted of perjury. Not only was he acquitted, the trial judge was quite critical of the Crown's case and clearly stated that he did not find the officer's conduct, notes or evidence given at the inquiry to be fabricated or the result of collusion with other officers. He went on to state that much of the officer's evidence was not substantially different than that of several of the other witnesses. While the Crown has refused to comment on the status of the other three officers, many experts are suggesting that the judge's decision and comments at this trial will likely result in charges being dropped against the other three officers.

health issues. He was talking loudly and irrationally but was not immediately threatening anyone. The manager advised that the man had ordered a meal but become upset when they would not serve him any alcohol.

The two deputies took over and began to use verbal and body language techniques to calm the subject. According to witnesses and the officer's own statements, the male did stop shouting but remained agitated and seemed unable or unwilling to respond logically or calmly. This went on for some time and the officers continued to use calming tactics. One of the officers went so far as to sit down at the table with the subject in an attempt to appear less intimidating. While the subject refused to accompany the officers outside, he did not appear to be aggressive and they did not immediately escalate use of force.

After several minutes it became evident to the officers that the male would not leave the premises voluntarily. One of the deputies, using a much firmer tone, told the subject that he would have to leave the restaurant. At that point the male became quite agitated. Both officers moved to take him by the arm and place him under arrest for causing a disturbance when, without warning, the subject suddenly bolted.

He ran towards the rear of the restaurant and as the two officers closed in on him, he grabbed a large unopened bottle of Evian water, which had been sitting on one of the tables, and threw it at them. Instead of striking the officers, the bottle flew past them and directly towards a table of seated customers. The officers immediately deployed a Taser, subdued the subject and placed him under arrest. Piercing screams from the table, however, made it evident the matter was not over. The bottle had struck a three-month-old child in the head. The injury was severe and the baby died a short time later in the hospital.

In spite of numerous witness statements from other customers and staff which were very supportive of the deputy's actions, the baby's parents subsequently sued the Sherriff's department and the two deputies, claiming that they had been negligent in not arresting the suspect sooner. The media were very critical of the police response and were quick to suggest that their delay of action had resulted in the death.

The internal investigation determined that the deputies could not have anticipated the suspect's actions and had taken the appropriate steps in terms of use and escalation of force. The lawsuit however went differently. The judge found that while the officers had not been wrong in how they dealt with the suspect, they had been negligent in not clearing or at least warning all of the customers, staff and bystanders away from the area.

While I certainly don't wish to challenge the judge's decision, it raises a concern that officers who are taking action based on standard operating procedures and experience can be second guessed and judged using the all seeing and all knowing power of hindsight in a situation that would be almost impossible to foresee!

Perfection is a wonderful goal but a crushing expectation.

5

POLICE USE OF FORCE

*Gentle people sleep safely in their beds at night
because rough men stand guard, bravely prepared
to do violence on their behalf.*

There are few things that generate more public criticism, disciplinary action and criminal charges than police use of force. From Rodney King, which sparked city-wide riots, to the Robert Dziekanski incident, which caused an international incident, police use of force is often the spark that ignites the forest fire and bears considerable discussion.

Police officers are tasked with the enforcement of the law, keeping of the peace and protection of the public. In turn, the public grants them specific powers, one being the entitlement to use force where it is necessary to fulfill those duties. In actual fact, this is often an uneasy contract.

The public expects and demands that officers use force only when necessary and only the minimum amount of force when it is applied. They often have unrealistic expectations based on their own perceptions which, in many cases, may be influenced by how television and movies portray use of force.

In real life, a struggle or fight between two reasonably matched individuals is violent, visceral, raw, terrifying and disgusting. There is nothing dignified or gentle about it and there is no way to make it look that way. The public may witness several officers physically and forcefully arresting a suspect and feel that it somehow offends the idea of fair play and that they are using excessive force. In reality, overwhelming force often prevents serious injury to offender and officer alike. They may view sanctioned police tactics such as baton strikes, come along techniques, compliance strikes or holds and use of pepper spray or Tasers as unnecessary and excessive. Finally, situations involving lethal use of force will and should come under intense public scrutiny, but will also usually involve much second guessing, criticism and condemnation, even in those cases that are clearly and totally justified.

Police officers are trained in the use of force. While training could, I suppose, vary from one department to the next, the generally accepted professional standard is to teach officers to use force only when necessary and in a progressive manner along a continuum from zero force to lethal force. This means that an officer may start with a simple, verbal instruction, issue a verbal warning, use gentle physical contact, move up to a higher level of physical contact, deploy a non-lethal weapon such as a baton, pepper spray or Taser and finally deploy a firearm or other lethal force.

One of the problems that can occur when the public witnesses police using force, in person or via a photo or video, is that in many cases they observe the final stages of the incident, thus missing much of the escalation that precipitated the use of force. The media, and internet sites such as YouTube, are willing and able to broadcast quickly and widely and this can clearly influence the public's perception of what occurred and affect their trust and faith in the police.

Public perceptions about police use of force is considerably influenced by any preconceived beliefs or expectations about the abilities of police officers, the effectiveness of their self-defense training and the weapons they have at their disposal for dealing with a threat. They have grown up with TV and movies showing police officers who are able to arrest multiple suspects with a few smooth moves and intricate holds. They see them disarm a knife wielding assailant with a single blow from fist or baton. They observe as officers fire a single, accurate shot from a sidearm, which not only instantly stops the suspect but flings him violently backwards. Police officers know that is not reality.

CASE STUDY:
One against four?

In 2009, four armed and physically fit male police officers from an urban police force in South America were called to the scene of an agitated male armed with a butcher knife. The police department had been attempting to arm their officers with Tasers but had not yet been able to do so. The following incident was videotaped by a local resident and is now used as a training video by the department.

Upon arrival the four officers spread out and surrounded the suspect so that he would be contained and offer no threat to the public. They were each approximately 10 to 15 feet from the suspect. None of them had their sidearm out and subsequent statements by the surviving officers revealed the reason was that they felt that might further enrage him. This turned out to be a tactical error.

As he was not immediately attacking, the officers attempted to engage him in a non physical and non threatening manner by using body language and verbal techniques. This seemed to be working until, without any warning, he attacked. The officers held their ground and attempted to un-holster their side arms. This turned out to be a second tactical error.

The suspect got to the first officer before a single firearm could even be drawn. He reached the second officer just as the first shots were fired. None of the first shots were fatal and while wounded, the suspect was actually able to get to and seriously wound the third officer. Then, in spite of having received lethal gunshot wounds, he was able to reach and inflict serious injuries to the fourth officer before finally succumbing to his injuries.

These officers were in a dangerous situation with few options available to them. With no intermediary device like pepper spray or Taser, the officers were forced to either use verbal skills or escalate to lethal force. Four trained and armed officers who surely felt they had the situation under control. That they were in little danger. And they were dead wrong...one dead officer and three seriously injured wrong.

CASE STUDY:
Surprise attack

In 2011, state troopers in Lafayette, Indiana attempted to stop a fleeing vehicle. After approximately four miles the driver lost control and the vehicle crashed into the ditch. The first two patrol cars on the scene stopped approximately 30 feet away and three officers exited with their firearms drawn. The dash mounted video camera in one of the police vehicles recorded what happened next.

With no warning and without any hesitation, the driver

exited the disabled vehicle and, armed with a large hunting knife, charged directly at one of the officers. In spite of the fact that these officers were on high alert and had weapons drawn, the suspect was able to cover almost the entire 30 feet before a single shot was fired. The officer he was threatening held his ground and fired at least two shots before the suspect reached him and stabbed him violently in the face. Before the suspect could inflict further damage, a volley of shots from the other two officers brought him down. The stabbed officer, although seriously injured, did survive.

In debriefings, all three of the officers expressed absolute and total surprise at how quickly the attack commenced and how rapidly the suspect was able to cover the distance. All three indicated that they had delayed in firing because none of them immediately recognized that he was armed with a knife. They also made note of the extreme challenge in firing accurately at a moving target while under extreme stress.

This was an unanticipated and illogical attack by a suspect who was intent, not on escaping, but on killing a police officer. Certainly these trained officers felt that they had left enough of a safety margin and would have ample time to react to whatever might occur, and therefore, that none of them were in danger. They were wrong.

RESEARCH ON KNIFE ATTACKS

In 1983 Sgt. Dennis Tueller, a police self-defense expert with the Salt Lake City Police Department, conducted a study using actual, trained officers (Tueller, 1983). His objective was to determine how far away a suspect armed with a knife or other lethal weapon had to be for a police officer to react, draw and fire their weapon. What he discovered was shocking even to the police world and has since become known as the Tueller 21' Rule.

Sgt. Tueller found that an alert police officer with no other distractions and who realized the attacker was armed would take 1.5 seconds to draw and fire their weapon. In the same time frame, an attacker could cover a distance of 21 feet. Even more alarming was that Tueller's experiment had the attacker stop the instant a shot was fired.

There have been many other experiments to support that shots fired while under intense stress are unlikely to be accurate. And, as some of the previous case studies have shown, it's also well demonstrated that a single shot is unlikely to be immediately fatal or stop the attacker instantly. Lastly, police are aware of many incidents, especially involving alcohol, drugs or mental illness, where mortally wounded subjects have covered astonishing distances and inflicted injury or death on the victim. Like many things in police work, an officer is forced to make the best situational decision they can and live or die on the outcome.

In 1992 Constable Darren Laur, a self-defense expert with the Victoria City Police, conducted an experiment using 85 trained police officers (Laur, 1992). His objective was to determine how an officer would react if attacked with a knife at close range. To achieve this, he armed an "attacker" with a chalked training knife. He then had each officer approach the attacker for routine questioning. The attacker was instructed that, mid-way through the contact, he was to pull the knife, yell, "I'm going to kill you" and immediately attack. What he discovered was hard to believe.

- 82 out of 85 never even saw or registered that the attacker had a knife on the initial attack.

- 72 out of 85 did not realize they were being repeatedly stabbed as opposed to being punched.

- 85 out of 85 received life threatening or fatal knife wounds (Based on chalk marks).

Closely related to the above research, noted self-defense instructors and authors of *Surviving Edged Weapons*, Dennis Anderson and Charles Remsberg, enlisted the assistance of Leo Gaje Jr. and Dan Inosanto; two of the top-rated, expert knife fighters in the world, and conducted several workshops and studies (Remsberg, 2012). They determined that there is almost no dependable hand-to-hand or baton defense against a determined attacker and that serious or fatal injuries were almost guaranteed to occur if a victim attempted to stand their ground and take defensive action.

They concluded that, without exception, the most successful defense in any knife attack is to defend yourself any way you can from lethal blows while doing everything possible to escape and flee from the attacker.

This is wonderful advice to any member of the public. But what if you are a police officer? What if it's your duty to stop the attacker? If you don't have the luxury of fleeing?

While I have focused on knives in these case studies, the same data really applies to other hand held weapons that could cause serious injury or death. Even lesser weapons such as penknives, small objects or yes, even an office stapler, can result in the loss of an eye. I don't think we should expect our officers to accept serious injury as part of their job description.

Knowing this information, the question must be asked, *how close is too close?* It creates an incredible dilemma for any officer. If they use lethal force too soon they are apt to be accused of executing or murdering the suspect. If they wait too long the suspect gets within the death radius and may kill or injure the officer or a member of the public.

Within the policing world, there are many stories told of almost super human feats carried out by suspects and officers who had sustained fatal wounds. This leaves most officers with less than one hundred percent confidence in the 21' rule. Incidentally, other subsequent studies have suggested that this distance may even be as much as 31 feet. Speaking personally, I much prefer something like a 50' rule...how about you?

FACTS ON USE OF FORCE

I have talked a great deal about how and why police use force, but to fully address it, we have to explore how wide spread it actually is, how frequently it really occurs and whether the public have cause to be alarmed.

Use of force concerns are reflected in the considerable attention and media coverage that accompanies allegations of police use of force, particularly if it is viewed as excessive. In many cases the real damage is done before any thorough investigation can be completed, thereby lumping unfounded accusations and allegations in with ones that actually occurred. This leads to an over-generalization and belief that police use of excessive force is rampant and out of control.

Police watchdog groups like civil liberties organizations often climb on the bandwagon and do their best to portray police and police departments as rogue, corrupt or violent. This again fosters a negative public mind set. In Canada, the BC Civil Liberties Union has been highly critical of police and the number of police involved deaths.

Because any police force must have the support and trust of the public to be effective, it is vitally important to understand the truth and the facts about police use of force. In this regard, I refer to statistics from the BC Coroner Service, the RCMP, a comprehensive study by Mark Henriquez, project manager for the National Police Use of Force Database Project at the International Association of Chiefs of Police and, in large part, to a huge study done by the US Department of Justice.

British Columbia Coroner Service Statistics

The BC Coroner Service is an independent body tasked with, among other things, holding inquests into all deaths of persons while in police custody or at the hands of the police. "In Custody" is considered to be any situation where police were present at or near the time of death or where the person was actually arrested and in custody or any person killed as a result of any police action or incident. This would include people who died from natural causes, suicide, alcohol or drug overdoses, motor vehicle accidents involving police, police chases, police negligence or police use of force.

This report showed that in a 15 year period, from 1992–2007 there were a total of 267 such deaths (MacAlister, 2010). While it does not break down the causal factors, a separate RCMP report determined that 80% of In Custody deaths were as a result of alcohol or drug overdoses. Again, there is no reliable data as to the number of deaths caused by police use of force, justified or other, but when one assumes that there are always a certain number of deaths due to natural causes, suicides, and accidents, it shows that in actual fact, there are very very few deaths at the hands of police, justified or otherwise.

If one were to add additional perspective, the Canadian Medical Association reports (Association, 2004) that every year in Canada, there are between 9,000–24,000 deaths within the medical community that are directly attributed to *preventable human error.*

Mark Henriquez Study:

In 1999, Mark Henriquez conducted a study into police use of force.(Henriquez, 1999). From 1994–98, his project documented 147,362 US-based incidents of police-related force, which resulted in 6,163 complaints, only 654 of which were sustained by independent review boards. He further determined that only .44% of force being used could be considered excessive.

US Department of Justice Study

In 1999, the US Department of Justice undertook a massive study of police use of force. It included thousands of officers from various departments across the country as well as a public questionnaire that sought the public's opinions and experiences with police (Justice, 1999).

1. It was determined that only 1% of police to public contact involved any use of force or threat of force. This was very consistent from one department to another and from one part of the country to another. It is actually remarkable in some ways when you consider the number of violent, emotional and volatile situations police are confronted with, the number of people police deal with who have substance abuse or mental health issues and the number of arrests and detentions officers are required to make.

2. It was discovered that almost *all* use of force by police officers occurred during an arrest and that the odds of force being used increased dramatically when suspects attempted to resist, flee, assault the officer, were using drugs, alcohol or were suffering from mental health issues. Researchers determined that in the case of substance abuse and mental health issues, the inability of the suspect to verbally engage with the officer in a rational or logical manner was a leading factor resulting in use of force.

3. The study examined 7,512 adult arrest records and found that less than one out of five involved any use of force outside that of handcuffing. In those cases where force was used, over 80% involved grabbing, pushing or holding that resulted in no injury at all. In the cases where there was injury reported, 48% were so minor in nature (bruising, abrasions) as to require no treatment. This means that in arrest situations, less that 2% of the arrests resulted in any injury greater than a bruise or abrasion!

4. Another very interesting concept they discovered in this study was what they referred to as "Subjective Objectivity." What they found is that different officers perceived the need and level of force differently. For example, a 55-year-old, 150 lb officer might view a threat level differently than 30-year-old, 220 lb. officer and might utilize the type and level of force in a different manner.

5. Interestingly, they found no statistical difference in use of force by female officers as compared to male officers.

6. Not surprisingly, they discovered that officers in high adrenaline incidents such as high speed chases, high risk arrests, and volatile situations were more likely to use force, including excessive force.

7. Closely related to this was the fact that officers who feared for their safety in a hostile crowd environment and felt the need to make a quick arrest and departure were more likely to use force and more apt to rapidly escalate the level of force.

There were two findings that can be of immense use to police departments and should be seriously considered by all senior management and training departments. First, is that a high percentage of police use of excessive force is committed by a very small minority of officers. In fact they referred to the well-known 80/20 factor where 80% of the complaints came from 20% of the officers.

The study did indicate that a great deal of care must be used when analyzing this type of data because there are several factors that can influence it. For example, an officer's assignments or duties can place them in a higher risk category as the type of crime and crime rate in the patrol area they are assigned to can have an effect. A proactive, hard working officer involved in many calls and arrests will have a higher likelihood of being involved in a use of force incident than an uninvolved, less active officer. To provide an example, one would expect that an officer assigned to Community Relations might have a significantly reduced chance of being involved in a use of force incident when compared to a patrol officer assigned duties in a high crime area.

So, while the actual number of use of force incidents by any particular officer may not be completely reliable, it should raise a warning flag and prompt a closer look. It may be nothing, but it may also be an officer who requires additional training, counseling, re-assignment or, in some cases, termination.

Given that virtually all use of force occurs during arrests, one method of investigating specific officers would be to obtain a record of their individual arrest records and compare the number of incidents of use of force to the number of arrests. It would also provide valuable information if an individual officer was involved in use of force *outside* of arrest situations.

The second finding, was that the researchers discovered that police to public contact was *transactional* in nature and that it involved input, actions and decisions from both parties. They reported that the final outcome was often pre-determined by the course of action an officer took *prior* to using force. Officers who acted and appeared unprofessional, used profanity or spoke in an aggressive, dismissive or insulting manner were much more likely to prompt a similar reaction from the person they were dealing with. This in turn tended to escalate the confrontation to the point where the officers were required to use force.

In other words, even though those officers were justified in using force, at the time they used it, the very circumstances which resulted in this justified use of force may have been caused or might have been prevented by the officers themselves.

If certain officers were found to be involved in higher than usual numbers of use of force incidents, departments might be well advised to investigate further. If it's determined that the officer's demeanor, attitude or approach is the cause of the problem, it might well be dealt with quickly with remedial training or some other form of action.

CASE STUDY:
Bad attitude

In 2009, two patrol officers working in a large US city were dispatched to a domestic disturbance. Upon arriving, they observed a small group of neighbors standing outside of the residence and they could hear loud shouting and screaming coming from inside. Both officers approached cautiously and when they got to the front door, they knocked and loudly identified themselves. The yelling stopped immediately and the door was opened by a large male. He had been drinking and was agitated, but responded well to the officer's presence and invited them in.

The younger officer began to speak with the husband and the older officer took the wife into another room to speak with her. It appeared that the fight had been strictly verbal and no physical assault had occurred. The younger officer had, by this time, calmed the husband completely down and convinced him that he should leave with the officers and stay the night at his parent's house. The situation seemed to be under control. It was at this point that the older officer returned.

He was visibly angry and began to berate the husband, calling him a coward and accusing him of being an abusive husband. He told the suspect he should be taken to jail and his children removed from his custody. The husband began to get upset and very agitated again. The younger officer attempted to regain control of the situation but the damage had been done. The verbal exchange became even more heated and the husband became so enraged that he attacked the older officer, striking him in the face, stunning and knocking him to the floor.

When the younger officer attempted to intervene, the husband threw him to the floor and again attacked the older officer. This time he grabbed a baseball bat that had been leaning against the couch and raised it as if to strike him. The younger officer drew his firearm and yelled at the husband to stop, but he was totally enraged by this time and began to attack. Having no other option, the young officer shot and killed the husband.

A husband dead. Two children left fatherless. And a young officer forced to live and deal with the aftermath of taking another human life. All because a police officer, who should have known better, acted in an unprofessional and unacceptable manner.

Was this shooting justified? Yes it was. But the real question is whether it could have been prevented or avoided. The answer to that is also, yes it could have. The actions of the older officer caused the situation to deteriorate and resulted in the tragic outcome.

Based on evidence from the wife, neighbors and the young officer, the police department determined that the older officer's conduct had resulted in the husband's death and in the endangerment of his partner and the public. This officer had been the subject of other complaints in the past and it was determined that he should be terminated. The young officer was fully vindicated by the department. He resigned one month later.

WHAT CAN WE LEARN?

There is a lot of good news in these studies for both the public and the police. I believe that governments, community leaders and police departments should be diligent in projecting these facts to the public. This might serve to combat negative and out of context comments or false reporting by the media and other self-serving groups or individuals with agendas harmful to the public-police relationship.

The police-public contract implies that the public will place their trust and faith in the police and the police will do their part to earn and honor that trust and faith. I believe that based on these reports, one can safely state the pact is unbroken.

I suppose that the Holy Grail for the police, when it comes to use of force, would be a device, not yet invented, that is fast and easy to deploy, will instantly incapacitate a suspect without any fear of injury or death and is 100% reliable. Every professional, well-intentioned police officer would welcome this, because in a perfect world, no police officer should ever have to put their hands on a suspect or risk injury to themselves or the public.

In the meantime however, police have to use the tools made available to them. In my opinion, the public should be very careful not to demand that police abandon techniques and tools just because they have resulted in rare cases of death or injury, because every tool or technique the police lose simply removes another option for the next time.

Consider this: In Canada, a recent study conducted by researchers Azedah Khalatbari of the University of Ottawa and Kouroush Jenab of Ryerson University examined 453 anesthesia related deaths that occurred over a nine month period. They reported that 80% of these deaths were as a direct result of human error. In spite of that, there is no public outcry demanding that doctors cease using anesthesia and return to giving the patient a shot of whiskey and a stick to bite on.

The question I have often grappled with and never resolved is: why do we hold law enforcement to such a different standard?

6

COMBAT STRESS SYNDROME

A little stress never killed anyone...but a lot just might!

In any examination that deals with the actions, decisions, judgment and memory of police officers involved in high stress or combat stress situations, the physiological and psychological effects of stress must be taken into account. This is especially true when you consider that many of the physical and emotional responses to high stress are involuntary and almost impossible to completely control.

Officers are expected to remain calm, under control, logical, rational and to be observant, with a detailed memory and recall of situations and events. Officers who fail in this regard are often highly criticized by public and peers alike. They may be accused of cover ups and lies and perhaps even worse. Some may feel guilty for having failed themselves, their colleagues and the public.

But have they failed, or have they simply been human?

PHYSIOLOGICAL FACTORS

Medical experts concur that when confronted with stressful situations, the sympathetic nervous system (SNS) releases stress hormones into the bloodstream and prepares the body for the well known *fight or flight* syndrome.

Heart and respiratory rates increase, pumping more oxygen and blood into the body. Blood moves from the extremities and towards the heart, lungs and brain. The limbic system, which controls emotions, is affected and the areas of the brain associated with long and short term memory are adversely affected. Skin and extremities become cold and clammy and fine muscle control becomes lessened. The pupils of the eye dilate, vision becomes more focused on the perceived threat and there is a diminished perception of pain.

In imminent danger situations, the portion of the brain controlling rational and logical thought process partially shuts down and is replaced by the portion of the brain that is instinctual in nature. Once the SNS is initiated, it will virtually dominate all voluntary and involuntary systems until the threat has been eliminated.

Psychological Factors

Almost everyone experiences stress in one form or another. In fact, entire industries are created to fulfill the human desire for thrills, fear and excitement. One only has to look at skydiving, contact sports, hunting and the hundreds of other activities designed for just this purpose. Experts agree that fear or excitement in and of itself is seldom the cause of acute stress. Even natural disaster events like earthquakes, floods and major storms cause minimal Post Traumatic Stress Disorder (PTSD) (Siddle, 2001).

What will consistently cause acute stress or PTSD is the "intentional, overt and close-range aggression, hostility or hatred from another human being." The Diagnostic and Statistical

Manual of the American Psychiatric Association affirms this when it notes that "Post-Traumatic Stress Disorder (PTSD) may be especially severe or longer lasting when the stressor is of human design."

Most human beings have a "phobia" level aversion to close range aggression, confrontation or hostility from another human and will go to great lengths to avoid or escape it. Police officers, on the other hand, have a duty and responsibility to face these situations frequently, and understanding the effects of this type of stress is critical if police and the public are to gain any insight into how police officers react and respond to critical incidents.

Bruce Siddle is an internationally recognized author and expert in what he refers to as "combat stress" involving Armed Forces and law enforcement personnel. He defines combat stress as being "the perception of an imminent threat of serious personal injury or death or the task of protecting another from imminent serious injury or death under conditions where time is minimal" and goes on to state that "the price of civilization is paid every day by police officers who are forced to engage in combat stress situations and the public rarely comprehends the magnitude of the psychological toll it takes" (Siddle, 2001).

Based on Siddle's interpretation of combat stress, the incident in question need not involve the use of lethal force but might include any type of incident where an officer perceives an imminent threat to themselves or others. This might include threats with any sort of weapon, or even without a weapon in some cases. Certainly it could include such things as police pursuits, riots or high risk searches and arrest situations.

The second part of what Siddle refers to as combat stress deals with an officer being forced to inflict serious injury or death on a fellow human being. He refers to a comprehensive study conducted by Brigadier General S. Marshall of the US military during World War II which found that in front line combat situations, only 20% of trained soldiers would actually fire their rifle at an enemy soldier. This percentage rose dramatically when applied to soldiers firing mortar rounds, machine guns, shooting from ships and planes or where individual targets were not selected but simply involved a point-and-shoot philosophy.

The natural aversion to hurting or killing a fellow human being was so strong that even combat soldiers in a war setting were reluctant to do so. When the results were published, the military changed the way it trained soldiers and among other things, went from paper "bulls eye" type targets to life-like targets that fell when hit. In the Korean War, the percentage of soldiers who would fire rose to 55% and by the Vietnam War it had risen to 95%.

As an interesting side report, researchers suggested that frequent exposure to combat-oriented video games involving life like targets that fell, bled or were blown up might well lead to desensitization or lessening of the normal aversion to killing that most humans have. Based on the above noted study, it certainly makes one wonder.

Siddle's studies indicate that in combat-style stress situations an officer may be literally "scared out of their wits" and explains that when the rational and logical thought process is diminished by the body's natural physiological reaction, the mammalian or instinct-based portion of the brain takes over. He states that this could well account for some cases where an officer uses excessive force, in that the instinctive reaction to extreme fear is to punish the person who caused the fear. In essence: *an instinctual desire to seek revenge for having been subjected to extreme fear.*

Might this explain those cases where an officer delivers the extra push, hit or kick to a suspect that is so often captured on video or witnessed by the public, precipitating accusations and even charges of excessive force? Would making officers aware of this information prepare or assist them in countering the reaction? I can't imagine it would hurt, and given the incredibly negative public reaction to police using excessive force, it certainly must be considered.

Critical Incident Amnesia

In 2001, Siddle teamed up with Lt. Col. D. Grossman of the US military to research what they refer to as *Critical Incident Amnesia* (Siddle, 2001). Grossman has conducted hundreds of studies, interviews and debriefings of military personnel involved in critical and combat incidents.

Their intent was to apply Grossman's findings to law enforcement personnel who were involved in critical or combat incidents. They felt that it might have significant importance since, in addition to a police officer's responsibility to respond instantly and appropriately to critical incidents, officers are also expected to accurately recall and report everything that occurs.

They reported that given the involuntary physiological reactions to such acute stress, memory impairment and reduced sensory input was inevitable. Both felt this reaction and the results posed one of the greatest challenges to individual officers, police departments and the public, who struggle to understand and cope with the aftermath of critical incidents.

By its very nature, acute stress affects memory recall of witnesses, victims, suspects and police officers and can result in failed investigations, failure to convict the guilty and sometimes in the persecution and prosecution of the innocent, including police officers.

Its effect is so profound that Siddle suggests that *every police officer, police department, police disciplinary board and prosecutor's office should be familiar with the implications of it as well as the procedures that might assist in dealing more appropriately with it* (Siddle, 2001).

These implications included:

1. A person's memory can be affected by that person's own experiences, expectations or pre-conceived beliefs.

2. Intense fixation on a threat will narrow the vision and thus the memory to the immediate, specific threat and may exclude peripheral details. This is often referred to as "tunnel vision" and can narrow the field of vision, and therefore memory, by as much as 70%.

3. Time and distance perception is altered leading to officers over or under estimating both.

4. Immediately after a critical incident the brain has not yet processed much of the information and will often result in a failure to recall the full detail of what was observed during the incident.

5. Inevitably the individual will seek additional information from any other source in an effort to make sense of what has occurred.

Siddle and Grossman believe that critical incident memory management is best achieved if standard procedures are implemented which will ensure the most accurate and complete memories are protected and preserved. Based primarily on studies conducted in the Military where combat action debriefings are common, and with the generally understood principle that *The first report is never right*, they recommend the following as practical standards:

1. Educate officers, police departments, prosecutors and even the public on the effects of critical stress on memory. This education and understanding is critical in reducing the guilt and confusion over memory loss and the potential for PTSD. Understanding and support of colleagues and supervisors is extremely important in how an officer will deal with the aftermath of a critical stress incident. Education may even influence how the public views the incident or in how disciplinary boards or prosecutors handle the situation.

2. Conduct a post incident interview as soon as possible following the incident. This should be a quick narrative report. It must be remembered that the person being interviewed will very likely fail to remember many of the events that actually occurred or their memory may simply be wrong. This is especially true when it involves space, distance, time or specific details outside the area of focus (tunnel vision). The initial interview should be recorded as the subject will likely be trembling or shaking as a result of the sympathetic nervous system's (SNS) effects on motor skills.

3. This initial interview should be conducted on an individual basis and steps should be taken to isolate the subject from other sources of information. Great care should be made not to influence the subject at this point through any suggestions, inferences or statements.

4. After the initial sleep period or approximately 24 hours later, the subject should be interviewed again and a written or taped statement taken. Again, it must be understood that the subject may add significantly to or change parts of their initial report and that is normal.

5. A group interview or debriefing should then be conducted as soon as practical after the secondary interviews. Additional memories may well surface in this setting as the subjects will receive certain retrieval cues from others. It has also been observed that subjects in a group debrief tend to be extremely frank, even at the expense of showing themselves in a poor light. This is attributed to the fact that colleagues are present and may well challenge the subject's version of events if their own recall is different.

6. The group debriefing should allow for each individual participant to completely relate their experience and observations. While there is certainly the potential for contamination of individual memories, it is slight, and in any event, the ultimate goal of the secondary debrief is to get as accurate and detailed an account of the entire critical incident as possible.

7. To be absolutely thorough, a second group debriefing should be held 48–72 hours after the incident. This allows some distance and sleep to have occurred and again, while the danger of memory contamination does exist, it is likely to be minimal, and the subjects may have been able to retrieve even additional memories.

8. Their recommendations include an acknowledgment that police officers are entitled to due process and the normal legal protections granted by the laws and policies of

various departments and regions and that this must be taken into account when statements are taken or debriefings conducted.

To lend further credibility to the findings of Siddle and Grossman, I have included portions of an article, *Practical Police Psychology*, published by PoliceOne.com and written by noted police psychologist Dr. Laurence Miller, Ph.D.

Dr. Miller is a clinical and forensic psychologist, law enforcement educator and trainer based in Boca Raton, Fla. He is the police psychologist for the West Palm Beach Police Department, mental health consultant for Troop L of the Florida Highway Patrol, a forensic psychological examiner for the Palm Beach County Court, and a consulting psychologist with several regional and national law enforcement agencies.

Perceptual, Cognitive, and Behavioral Disturbances

Most officers who have been involved in a high threat episode have described one or more alterations in perception, thinking, and behavior that occurred during the event. Most of these can be interpreted as natural adaptive defensive reactions of an organism's nervous system to extreme emergency stress.

Most common are *distortions in time perception*. In the majority of these cases, officers recall the event as occurring in slow motion, although a smaller percentage report experiencing the event as speeded up.

Sensory distortions are common and most commonly involve tunnel vision, in which the officer is sharply focused on one particular aspect of the visual field, typically, the suspect's weapon, while blocking out everything in the periphery. Similarly, "*tunnel hearing*" may occur, in which the officer's auditory attention is focused exclusively on a particular set of sounds, most commonly the suspect's voice, while background sounds are excluded. Sounds may also seem muffled or, in a smaller number of cases, louder than normal. Officers have reported not hearing their own or other officers' gunshots.

Some form of *perceptual and/or behavioral dissociation* may occur. In extreme cases, officers may describe feeling as though they were standing outside or hovering above the scene, observing it "like it was happening to someone else." In milder cases, the officer may report that he or she "just went on automatic," performing whatever actions he took with a sense of robotic detachment. Some officers report intrusive distracting thoughts during the scene, often involving loved ones or other personal matters, but it is not known if these substantially affected the officers' actions during the event.

A sense of helplessness may occur during a high threat episode, but may be underreported due to the potential stigma attached. A very small proportion of officers report that they "froze" at some point during the event: either this is an uncommon response or officers are understandably reluctant to report it. In a series of interviews by police psychologist Dr. Alexis Artwohl, most of these cases seemed to represent the normal *action–reaction gap* in which officers make the split-second judgment call to shoot only after the suspect has clearly threatened someone's life. This brief evaluative interval is actually a positive precaution to prevent the premature shooting of a nonthreatening citizen. But in cases where the otherwise prudent action led to a tragic outcome, this hesitation may well be viewed retrospectively as a fault: "If I hadn't waited to see him draw, maybe that store owner would still be alive."

Disturbances in memory are commonly reported in high threat cases. About half of these involve impaired recall for at least some of the events during the incident; the other half involve impaired recall for at least part of the officer's own actions — this latter reaction may be associated with the "going-on-automatic" response. More rarely, some aspects of the scene may be recalled with unusually vivid clarity — *a flashbulb memory.*

Over a third of cases involve not so much a loss of memory as a distortion of recall, which may cause the officer's account of what happened to differ markedly from the report of other observers at the scene.

An administrative implication of this cognitive phenomenon is that discrepant accounts among eyewitnesses to a critical incident scene should not necessarily be interpreted as one or more persons lying or consciously distorting his report, but may well represent honest differences of perception and recall.

CASE STUDY:
Conflicting stories

In February 2005, police on patrol in a Chicago residential area heard what they believed to be a gunshot and at the same time observed a van proceeding the wrong way down a one way street with its lights off. The two officers called for back-up and followed the vehicle for several blocks until the other two officers arrived, at which time they pulled it over. It was at this point that the sequence of events began to fragment based on whose version was told after the incident.

The suspect's version of events was that he was stopped and physically pulled from his vehicle by the officers who tried to restrain him while he sought to produce his identification. When one of the officers found a gun in his waistband, he shouted "gun" and tried to remove it from his possession. At this point the officers all opened fire and the suspect returned fire in self defense.

An 18-year-old independent witness said that she had been locked out of her house that night and observed as two police cars stopped the van. She says she saw police officers "snatch" the suspect from the van and eventually shoot him. She testified that the suspect had his hands behind his back when the officers started shooting and that they continued to shoot at him as he lay on the ground. She also advised that she had seen a female police officer seated in the rear of one of the police vehicles. It should be noted that her testimony at trial was significantly different from her written statement given to police soon after the incident and in fact there had not been any other officer at the scene, male or female.

The officers advised that when the suspect exited the van, he was ordered to place his hands on the side of the van. He initially complied but then began to struggle while being searched. The officers reported that he began to pull a gun from his waistband and that one of the officers yelled, "gun!" The suspect dropped to the ground and began to fire what was a total of 17 shots, striking three of the officers in the arms and legs. The officers all returned fire from different positions and directions, striking the suspect in the neck, back and legs. The suspect was struck a total of 28 times. Incredibly, he survived.

During the subsequent investigation and court testimony, much was made of the different versions of events. In truth, even the evidence and statements of the individual officers varied in many regards, most specifically in details as to each other's locations, number of shots fired, the time frame involved, when they stopped shooting and whether the suspect was on his back or his stomach during the incident. There was much public and media criticism that the suspect had received shots in the back. The officers tried to explain that not only were they firing from different angles and locations, but the suspect himself was moving and twisting as he fired. The media reports continued to be quite harsh and accused the officers of lying and making misleading statements, suggesting that the lack of recall and the differing versions was somehow proof of deception.

Given what we know about Critical Incident Amnesia and stress, it should be no surprise that there were differing versions of events from all parties. It would be more surprising if there were not. It might well be said however, that most in the public or media are not familiar with this syndrome and thus fail to understand its implications and impact. This of course leads to skepticism, suspicion and distrust.

In this case, and in spite of media reports and a huge campaign by the Alliance Against Racist and Political Repression to turn the incident into one about race, the suspect was convicted and sentenced to 40 years in prison.

CASE STUDY:
Extreme focus

In late May, 2007, police in Yakima, Washington were called to a complaint of shots fired and upon attending found the body of Juan Ramos. He had been shot five times. Investigation revealed that the suspect was one Jose Alvarez and a warrant was issued for his arrest.

On June 8, police observed the suspect in a green Tahoe and attempted to stop him. He abandoned the vehicle in an alley and attempted to flee on foot. As officers closed in on the area, Officer Illeana Salinas observed Alvarez running down the street. When he saw her he veered off the road and jumped over a low fence with Officer Salinas pursuing him on foot. She advised that he was wearing a tight white muscle shirt and dark pants and she could not see any weapon. She tried to notify dispatch of her location but radio traffic was high and she was not certain that she had gotten through.

A short ways down the alley, Officer Salinas caught the suspect and attempted to physically apprehend him. Alvarez began to struggle and Officer Salinas attempted to restrain him by putting him in a head lock using her right arm. It was at this point that she observed the suspect pull a handgun from his waistband and attempt to shoot her. As she was using her strong right arm to hold him, she was unable to draw her own weapon and all she could do was to keep pushing Alvarez's weapon away with her left hand as he continued to try pointing it at her.

Officer Salinas advised that as she began to lose control of Alvarez, she realized that her only hope was to release him, try to put as much distance between them as she could and then attempt to draw and fire her own weapon. Salinas said she knew that she would almost certainly be shot and mentally prepared herself for that. She then pushed Alvarez away from her and at the same time ran several steps away while drawing her weapon. Just as she was turning, she heard a gunshot.

She completed her turn and observed Alvarez on the ground. Although she couldn't feel any pain, she was certain that she had been struck. She fired one round at Alvarez before realizing that he had already been shot. As other officers arrived on the scene, Salinas was so convinced she'd been shot that she asked them to check her over for gunshot wounds. She was trembling and clearly suffering from the after effects of extreme adrenaline and stress. She expressed extraordinary anger at Alvarez and can recall being almost irrationally upset that he had attempted to kill her.

In the debriefing, it became clear what had actually happened. As Alvarez had been fleeing, he was also being pursued on foot by another officer. Officer Sam Masters arrived just in time to observe Officer Salinas physically disengage from the suspect. He observed the weapon and yelled that he had a gun. As Alvarez began to turn and raise his weapon, Officer Masters fired one shot which struck the suspect in the head, killing him.

Officer Salinas provided her post incident statement and advised that while chasing Alvarez and then during the struggle with him, she had experienced total auditory and visual exclusion, meaning that she did not hear or see anything beyond the suspect and his weapon. She did not hear the approaching sirens, she did not see or hear Officer Masters and in fact was absolutely convinced that she had been shot and that the shot had come from Alvarez. She had literally blanked out everything in the surrounding area except the immediate threat posed by Alvarez and his weapon.

The members of Alvarez's family were very upset and complained to local media that he had been the victim of racist and "trigger happy" police.

Officer Salinas and Masters were cleared and the shooting deemed a justified use of force. Both officers returned to work within 30 days.

These reports and studies reveal and discuss several very important issues. The scientific understanding of memory process and the effects of critical stress both physiologically and psychologically, when applied to law enforcement, is invaluable from many different aspects. It will result in more accurate eye-witness accounts from the public and the police.

It also forms the basis for an understanding of how police officers can give a version of events that seemingly conflicts with other evidence. It assists officers in dealing with the guilt and shame of failed memory. And it may ultimately assist the public in maintaining the trust, faith and support that forms one part of the police–public contract.

7

POLICE MISCONDUCT

The bad, criminal or unprofessional behavior of another officer reflects poorly on the entire department and every officer feels that very keenly.

Much has been said about police investigating police and how it should not be allowed due to the conflict of interest. Frankly, I agree, but not for the same reason as many of the critics. I have personally done several "internal" investigations and seen many others. In almost every case the police are as hard if not harder on their own. It's difficult for one police officer to con another, and in my experience, no police officer wants a bad apple on the force or in the department.

The bad, criminal or unprofessional behavior of another officer reflects poorly on the entire department and every officer feels that very keenly. When an officer reads or hears in the local media about a police officer who has committed a crime, they know full well how that news will be used by some to taunt, mock or humiliate them. They know that some may use it to make false accusations against other officers and that it erodes the public trust and support necessary for them to carry out their duties.

I don't agree with police investigating police because of the public's *perception*. When police investigate police there is only one outcome that will *not* result in calls of cover up or bias, and that is a finding of guilt and the laying of charges. Any other finding, regardless of the facts, will be called a cover up.

Why does the media and public seem so convinced that there is a "blue wall of silence" and that police officers will protect their own, circle the wagons or maintain some code of silence no matter what? Perhaps, in part, because there is a misconception about how police handle complaints and allegations.

I believe, however, that another factor plays a very large part. That's the fact that many incidents or complaints receive wide, initial public or media attention, which focuses solely on the allegation, and then fades away before the final results are published. This simply ignores the fact that many investigations determine that the complaints and allegations were either totally false, were unsupported by sufficient evidence or found that the officer took justified and supportable action. . .*because that is the way it really was.*

Police officers, like the general public, are entitled to due process and a presumption of innocence. Just because an allegation is made doesn't make it true. Just because an incident appears a certain way doesn't mean it was that way. Surely we don't expect a police officer to be sacrificed on the altar of public opinion so that the public and media are appeased?

In fact, every police force must take great care that this is *not* allowed to happen. If the media and public want to call that police protecting police then so be it.

This does raise an interesting point. When police officers are accused of misconduct, police departments are placed in a very precarious position. On the one hand, they are accountable to the public and must take public sentiment into account. On the other hand, they owe a duty to their employees and must ensure they are treated fairly and with due process. If management is seen to abandon an employee at the first sign of trouble, they will lose the trust and confidence of all other employees, and this must be prevented. The dilemma of course, is that when police departments don't immediately condemn the accused officer, they appear to be protecting or even supporting them and the public perception will be that they are protecting their own, covering up or refusing to be accountable.

Many police forces and departments have their own Internal Affairs or Professional Standards units tasked with investigating allegations made about police officers. While television and movies often portray these units as being universally hated and despised by police officers, this is largely a myth, and, like many myths, contributes to generalizations and misconceptions. In actual fact, I had many friends who served in internal investigation units. Without exception, they were well accepted and respected police officers who took their job function seriously and conducted investigations impartially and thoroughly.

In almost every case of police involved deaths or serious injury, or any criminal conduct where even a minimal amount of evidence exists, police departments refer the file to the Crown counsel, DA or prosecutor for an independent, third party review. Certainly in Canada, the final decision regarding criminal charges rests primarily with the Crown counsel or the prosecutor and in my opinion this should suffice to appease the public demand for impartiality and fairness.

Not surprisingly, my opinion has failed to sway the public sentiment, and many jurisdictions and departments have deferred even the investigation of such offences to an independent investigative body. The question this raises is, where will these independent units find experienced investigators with the skills, knowledge and experience to properly conduct investigations?

Investigations that will involve interviewing witnesses and police officers, collection and handling of evidence for court purposes and many other investigative skills and techniques that police officers spend years developing. I wonder how someone who has little experience or training in interviewing techniques will fare when interviewing a police officer who may have personally conducted hundreds of such interviews. I suppose that is something that every independent investigative unit will have to deal with through staffing and training.

In any event, when all is said and done, I think that most police officers welcome an independent external investigative organization, as it removes any hint or perception, however unfounded, of undue or improper bias. Whether it turns out to be appearance trumping effectiveness remains to be seen.

In order to discuss the topic of police misconduct, one must make a distinction between criminal behavior, departmental corruption, duty related misconduct and non duty related misconduct. Clearly each of these categories will contain a wide range of behaviors that will vary greatly in substance and seriousness. In addition to this, we must also discuss the unfounded and unproven accusations and allegations that often contribute to the public perceptions that surround issues of police misconduct.

Deliberate Criminal Behavior

This is likely to be the most serious of misconduct issues that confront police officers and police departments and, very fortunately, is also one of the least frequent. I don't personally know of any police officers who would knowingly ignore, condone or protect another officer who is involved in deliberate criminal behavior. In fact, I can think of no case in my 21 years of policing where that occurred.

Certainly I have heard of and even known officers who committed criminal acts. And the very reason I have heard of them is because these officers were apprehended and charged by other, honest and professional police officers.

I can say with certitude that in every case that I'm aware of, where an officer has been arrested and convicted of a deliberate criminal offence, they have been shunned and totally ostracized by other police officers. Even, and perhaps especially, by those who had been personal friends and co-workers. This is quite understandable when one considers the magnitude of such a betrayal. To have a friend or a co-worker offend everything you have dedicated and even risked your life to defend and protect is unforgivable. As with most things in life, the ones we know and care about have the greatest ability to cause hurt, and police officers are no different.

When police officers are suspected of committing criminal acts on or off duty, every effort is made to bring them to justice. If found guilty, they should face the same consequences as any other citizens and if officers use their position in law enforcement to commit the crime, they should face additional charges for breach of public trust.

There is virtually no disagreement about this amongst individual police officers. I have never been a member of a police union and can't comment with any reliability about them, but I would strongly suggest that while one of the union's functions is the protection of its members, no union or union member would or should wish to see a police officer avoid accountability for deliberate criminal acts.

Police Corruption

For our purposes here, corruption would refer to such things as bribery, planting of evidence, giving false evidence, protection rackets, supplying confidential information to criminals, drug or weapons trafficking, blackmail, extortion or any other similar activities that are conducted in an organized, systemic manner and involve multiple police officers working together, or independently, with the knowledge and support of others.

Thankfully, in modern day North American police forces, this type of activity is very rare. While some individual officers have committed such crimes over the years, the largest case of alleged police corruption in Canada was in the 1990s when five Toronto police drug squad officers were charged with multiple crimes involving police corruption related activities. While it can be said that nothing about police corruption is good, if the worst case of police corruption in the history of Canada only involved 5 officers and took place over a decade ago, we can take some comfort in knowing how small and rare the problem really is.

I would suggest the same applies to the US relative to population. There are simply too many checks and balances, too much public scrutiny and too much freedom and exchange of information for this to occur in any but the most isolated of cases.

Duty-related Misconduct

This type of complaint is by far the most frequent and perhaps because of that, the most damaging to the reputations of individual officers and police departments. It can involve anything from an officer being rude to a citizen to an officer using lethal force.

In some cases the behavior is so clearly improper, excessive or unprofessional, that there is no doubt and little defense. In those cases, discipline should be swift and appropriate, taking into account the due process of the individual department. It is the gray areas that are the most difficult to resolve.

Because so much of what an officer does is based on judgment and on-scene assessments, it can be almost impossible to accurately balance the protection of the officer with the protection of the public. In essence we are dealing with the Subjective Objectivity dilemma again.

For example, a physical altercation might occur where the suspect is thrown to the ground and breaks an arm. Was this excessive or was the broken arm the unintended consequence of a justified action? When a suspect appears to be under the control of officers and yet receives another strike or kick was it an accepted control tactic or excessive force? If a baton strike aimed at a shoulder misses and accidently impacts the head, is that excessive force or an accident resulting from a justified action? If a 220 lb 6'4" officer strikes a suspect with a baton to subdue them, it might well be considered excessive. If a 125 lb. 5'1" officer does the same perhaps it's not.

What if an officer observes and stops a car containing four African Americans late at night driving through a predominately Caucasian area? Is that racial profiling? What if they stop four Caucasians cruising late at night in a predominately African American area? Is that racial profiling? Or are both simply a case of officers observing and responding to something that is out of place or out of character? Could it be based on information they had about problems or suspects involved with drug dealing, prostitution or other crime in those respective areas?

When officers become frustrated or angry and use abusive, profane language they demean themselves, their colleagues and their departments. There is little excuse for this type of behavior and it is very damaging to the professional reputation of all parties. Having said that, it might be slightly more understandable if used during a violent incident that generated fear or anger and where an officer was instinctively reacting to or expressing that fear or anger.

In each of the situations noted above, there may be several different explanations, perceptions and opinions. Certainly one of them might simply be that the officer acted badly, showed poor judgment, was unprofessional, abusive or excessive. But that is certainly not always the case and police officers, like the public, should be given the benefit of the doubt.

Non-duty Related Misconduct

As with other forms of misconduct, there is a wide range of behavior that can be contemplated. In terms of criminal behavior, officers involved in criminal behavior should be treated exactly the same as any other citizen without fear or favor. I would be surprised if there was much dissent over this, with the exception that some will feel that a police officer should be held to a higher standard and perhaps receive more severe treatment by the courts. My personal opinion is that they should not, so long as the criminal behavior is not in any way assisted or bolstered by the officer's job or position in law enforcement. If it is, additional charges may well apply.

As usual, the real problem stems from balancing those behaviors that fail to meet the public's standards and expectations and the right of an officer to have a normal personal life while off duty. In this area I believe that an officer must be allowed the same standards and types of behavior that any other citizen might enjoy or be allowed without having it affect their career.

Police officers might be unfaithful spouses, indifferent parents, inconsiderate neighbors, or have poor social graces and still be good, effective police officers. The police do not hold themselves out to be the "morals police" or the "social graces police" and police departments should allow significant latitude in off duty related incidents. A caveat to that would be that no officer should be allowed, by comment or action, to represent or associate their police department to off duty behavior or conduct without the consent of the department. If there are any civil remedies that deal with certain behaviors, citizens who complain should be so advised and directed.

Having said all of this, it is certainly a great benefit to police officers and departments when officers comport themselves with honor, dignity and grace both on and off duty and frankly, most officers do exactly that.

When discussing the public's theory that police protect their own, two things come to mind. Firstly, I will say that on duty misconduct by officers probably generates the most inter-departmental colleague sympathy and understanding of all.

Fellow officers have been in physical and verbal altercations many times. They are aware that not every officer will be immune to anger or frustration on every occasion. That day-to-day behavior can be affected by many factors and that sometimes an outcome is much different than what was intended. They know that the application of force is not a science. That excessive force can even be accidental in nature and that in every case it can be almost impossible to gauge precisely. In fact, other officers may well adopt an attitude of *there but for the grace of God go I…*and be reluctant to formally report or stand witness to it.

This might be expected to be especially true in the more minor incidents. Many such incidents are dealt with informally, colleague to colleague or perhaps supervisor to subordinate and never becomes an issue again. Those officers who persist in that type of behavior are much more likely to be reported by fellow officers and dealt with formally.

Secondly, because of the difficulty in determining and considering all of the various factors, degrees and judgments involved with many misconduct complaints and then balancing that with the importance of preserving the officer's right to due process, it is inevitable that many such investigations will result in a finding of innocence, justification, or insufficient or inconclusive evidence. Naturally, that in turn can lead to a negative public reaction and accusations of cover up, blue walls of silence, police protecting their own or even corruption.

One thing that every department should consider are the benefits of having officers wear some sort of small microphone which would transmit and record to a unit in the police vehicle or main station. In my opinion, there are several positive aspects of this.

It would eliminate the "he said she said" element of many public complaints about police officers. It would provide an accurate recording of any statements, warnings or commands made to or by police. It would likely prevent officers from making gratuitous, unprofessional comments. Lastly, it would provide supervisors an opportunity to review or monitor how officers were interacting with the public in terms of what action, advice or comments were being made and, where necessary, intercede for the purpose of providing remedial training, guidance, or advice.

While some officers may view this as intrusive, there is little doubt that in the vast majority of situations a recording would vindicate the officer, assist them in completing reports or notes, and in general, be a positive policing tool.

CASE STUDY:
Getting the record straight

In 2011, a State trooper in Louisiana decided that he would purchase and carry a recording device which he'd activate during every traffic stop. Several weeks later he had occasion to stop a male driver for speeding. The driver was upset and made the usual comments about police having more important things to do, but he was not unduly rude and departed once the ticket had been issued.

Immediately after the encounter, the male drove directly to the police station and asked to speak with the trooper's superior. He then stated that the officer had made an unwarranted and uninvited sexual advance on him and he wished to make a formal complaint.

When questioned, the trooper had the taped transcript of the entire interaction from first to last contact. As a result, not only was he fully vindicated but the District Attorney laid a criminal charge against the driver.

CASE STUDY:
Policing our own

In 1995 an RCMP audit discovered that cash seized during a major drug investigation was missing from the secure exhibits locker located at RCMP HQ in Vancouver, BC. A major investigation was undertaken using Internal Investigations and the BC Major Crimes Section. There were several theories as to what may have occurred and who may have been responsible but nothing prepared many of us for the identity of the suspect.

After a lengthy investigation involving surveillance and other advanced investigative techniques, including a sting type strategy, a suspect was arrested and identified as one of the most highly respected drug section officers in the entire country. In fact, at the time of his arrest, he was working as a consultant for a UN country and was recognized internationally as an expert in his field.

I had known this officer personally for years. I had known his brother, also a respected officer, for many years. The news was little short of devastating. I clearly recall the shame I felt even though I had no involvement. I recall the bewilderment and even grief of other officers who had known and respected this man. And I recall the utter humiliation of this officer's brother.

The suspect was charged with a variety of offences and while out on bail was required to "sign in" at the front desk of the detachment where I worked. He could not or would not meet anyone's eye or acknowledge anyone he had known for years, including me.

Interestingly, nobody else, including me, made any effort to engage this officer, to sympathize, console or even acknowledge him. He had brought shame to himself, his family, his colleagues and his police force. He had breached the public trust and in doing so had destroyed any good will, past deeds or reputation he had achieved over a career spanning 28 years.

He was subsequently sentenced to time in prison and I have never heard of any officer visiting him there. He had achieved the complete and total destruction of his career and reputation.

CASE STUDY:
One bad apple

In Nov 2012, a suspect entered a branch of the Bank of America in San Francisco, brandished a weapon and handed the teller a note which said that he had a gun and wanted cash. The suspect then fled on foot with $1700 cash. San Francisco Police Department conducted the investigation and obtained a copy of the bank's surveillance video. They released the video to the public and a short while later received information that every police officer and department dreads. The suspect was a SF police officer.

Another SF police officer had been at home watching television when he noted the video on the news. He reported that his attention was first drawn when he noticed the manner in which the suspect handled the weapon. He felt that it resembled how police officers were trained to hold and handle a weapon when they do not want an accidental discharge. He then noted the suspect's stance and walk and that, in combination with other physical clues, convinced him that he recognized the suspect as another SF police officer. He immediately reported the matter and investigators, acting on this information, recovered the robbery note. As a result of fingerprints and other evidence, they arrested a 36-year-old SF police officer for the robbery.

"San Franciscans expect the men and women in uniform to uphold the laws and protect our residents," the district attorney was quoted as saying. "This officer's conduct is deplorable and will be met with serious consequences."

A letter written by a fellow officer was posted on a police web site. In short, it stated, "Thank you, you scumbag, for making a disgrace of the badge. Thank you for insulting every honest cop in the country. Thank you for giving our citizens cause to believe that police officers can't be trusted. It's officers such as myself that battle with that every day, knowing that to some, I'm going to be painted with the same brush as you. It's my greatest hope that you spend a long time in jail. As for me, I intend to remember you only as a good example of a bad cop."

CASE STUDY:
Perceptions of sexual harassment

I was once assigned an internal investigation regarding a complaint that had been made by a worker at the rape crisis center alleging that an officer had sexually assaulted a woman. This was an incredibly serious accusation and required immediate action so I quickly arranged an interview with the victim.

She arrived at the office accompanied by the rape crisis worker. Initially upon arriving in the interview office, the crisis worker began trying to provide me with the details of the incident and was somewhat aggressive when I advised her that it was critical that I speak directly and solely with the victim. I advised them that it was the victim's choice as to whether the worker was present or not but that I had to ask her to remain silent, at least until the interview was concluded. The victim elected to have the worker remain and I began the interview.

In condensed form, her statement specified that she had first met the officer when he attended to a complaint of a domestic dispute involving her and her boyfriend. It had not involved violence and nobody was arrested, but the victim decided to end the short relationship anyway and the boyfriend voluntarily moved out.

A few days later the officer called her again to follow up and ask if she was doing okay. At that time they engaged in a short conversation which was totally professional in nature. The victim then stated that several days after the second contact, the officer called her while off duty and they agreed to meet for a coffee. This eventually led to a consensual, romantic relationship between the two which lasted approximately two months.

During this time the officer confined their contact to his off duty hours and did not act inappropriately in any manner. After approximately two months the officer terminated the relationship and the victim was hurt and angry. She discussed the matter with the crisis worker who felt that the officer had used his position as a police officer to take advantage of her vulnerability and coerce her into the relationship.

Once the interview was concluded the crisis worker made it very clear that they both considered what had occurred as a sexual assault and were insistent that charges be laid or at the very least discipline meted out.

I subsequently interviewed the officer and his version of events was similar up to the point of the inappropriate coercion allegation which he adamantly refuted.

The dilemma here, was that based on both victim and officer version of events, there was clearly no criminal offence of sexual assault. It did however raise the issue of whether it was appropriate for an officer to have a personal relationship with a person they had met through work and whether or not that relationship was in fact coercive in nature. In analyzing this, the Force had to assess if the officer was in any counseling role with the victim, held a position of authority over the victim or, as a police officer, was in control of any aspect of the victim's life.

It was determined that the officer did not fill any such role in the victim's life, that the relationship was consensual and that there were many people in society who met through or at their work. The matter was concluded as being a complaint without substance.

There is little doubt that both the complainant and the Crisis worker felt that the findings were not appropriate and that the police had covered up and protected their own. The simple truth, however, is that this was a case where the victim's and the crisis worker's perceptions, personal biases and expectations varied significantly from the facts and evidence.

To repeat a point made earlier, we should not be willing to sacrifice an officer simply to appease public perception. So long as investigations are thorough and unbiased, the public need has been satisfied. Even if not fully appreciated or understood!

8

DISCIPLINE OF POLICE OFFICERS

If discipline means to teach, guide, mold, train, change or punish...let punishment be the last and least used.

Every society, and almost all organizations within that society, requires a system of discipline in order to operate and function with some semblance of order and efficiency. It's curious to note that discipline has several meanings, and while the most common refers to punishment, it also means instruction, guidance, teaching and training. In society, the legal system attempts to fulfill this role.

In most large organizations, there are provisions for discipline and fairly strict procedures for how it may be applied. Most involve some degree of progressive application which might range from an unofficial verbal discussion to termination.

All disciplinary process should be comprehensive, fair, consistent and swift. In almost all cases the employee should have an opportunity to challenge or appeal the discipline and this due process should be intended to provide a fair, unbiased application. Clearly, the goal for any organization would be that teaching, guidance and training be the first course of action and that discipline as punishment would be the last resort and the least used.

In many typical occupations, an employee's behavior, production, attitude and quality of work can be fairly easily monitored and quantified. For example, being late for work is easily noted and judged. Failing to complete work assignments on time, low production and subpar performance is generally easy to assess. Certainly any violence, physical or verbal altercations or criminal activity has no place in the normal workplace and would be considered totally unacceptable.

What does make police departments different is the very subjective nature of many of the actions and decisions that an officer deals with; the confrontational, emotional and violent situations they are called to attend and the many different levels and options of force that can be deployed.

In an effort to examine the different aspects of police discipline, it's necessary to discuss the various levels of seriousness and deal with each separately. Many of the suggestions and opinions expressed are closely related to the disciplinary standards of other large organizations, both private and public. They also echo many of the same guidelines and policies which are currently being practiced by a number of large police departments.

MINOR INTERNAL INFRACTIONS

Like other organizations, police departments are comprised of many different people with different abilities, work ethics and attitudes. Officers can be late for work or produce work that is of poor quality. They might act carelessly, cause turmoil in the workplace or partake in a host of other minor types of misbehaviors common to most large organizations.

No organization should allow itself to be bogged down and rendered inefficient over relatively minor disciplinary matters and should take all steps to ensure that discipline is meted out fairly and quickly.

Appeals should be dealt with fairly and quickly. Discipline which is improperly applied or appeals which are frivolous or vexatious in nature should not be tolerated. Whenever possible, mediation should be attempted for the resolution of disputes, especially in minor incidents, with the goal being a mutually agreed upon conclusion to the matter.

Line supervisors such as unit and detachment commanders should be provided with as many options as possible and allowed significant latitude to deal with these types of minor discipline problems. This might include everything from remedial training or unofficial warnings to unpaid suspensions of short duration. As stated earlier, the primary consideration at this level should be more developmental than punitive.

If appealing, an officer should have a very limited time to do so. At this level, the appeal should be dealt with quickly by the first level of senior management. In the case of the RCMP this might be an Inspector or Superintendent. When appropriate, mediation should be considered. There should be no appeal beyond that.

This ensures that the discipline was fairly applied, the employee had an opportunity to appeal and the entire matter is dealt with in a matter of days, allowing all parties to move forward and concentrate on the job at hand.

SERIOUS INTERNAL INFRACTIONS

This type of behavior might include more serious breaches of department policy, such as insubordination, harassment of co-workers, negligence, code of conduct infractions, inappropriate use of force or any other behavior that is serious in nature but has not reached the status of major or criminal.

The levels of discipline might range from a formal written warning, mandatory training or treatment or longer term suspensions with or without pay, but not termination. The authority to levy this degree of discipline should be delegated to the rank or supervisory level of senior management.

Any appeal should be allowed a reasonable period of time to prepare and should be heard by a senior officer such as the commanding officer, deputy chief or a very senior delegate. In some cases there may be internal or external appeal or hearing boards. Again, there should not be any further appeal beyond that.

MAJOR INTERNAL INFRACTIONS

This type of behavior would be of the nature that would require significant discipline in the form of lengthy unpaid suspensions, demotions or termination but has not reached the level of criminal.

This might include employees who knowingly falsified reports, misled or lied to supervisors, refused to obey orders, sexually harassed or bullied co-workers, continually failed to respond to lower levels of discipline or made unauthorized, public comments showing disloyalty or disrespect to co-workers, supervisors or the police department.

This level of discipline should be meted out by very senior levels of management such as C/Superintendant or Deputy Chief with appeals heard by an approved disciplinary board of officers or management above the level or rank of the one who initially meted out the discipline. A final appeal to the commissioner, chief of police or independent appeals board should be allowed.

CRIMINAL BEHAVIOR

This type of behavior often involves two very separate transactions. There will be a criminal investigation done for the purposes of a prosecution in court and more often than not a parallel, internal investigation for the purposes of determining what, if any, internal breach of discipline occurred and if so, what the appropriate response should be. Levels of internal discipline could be determined using the same process as for Major Internal.

The criminal process, including appeal, is in the hands of the justice system and is totally outside the influence of the employer or the employee.

APPLICATION OF DISCIPLINE

Properly applied and timely discipline has many positive effects on all parties, including the disciplined employee, co-workers and supervisors. It also impacts how the department is viewed and supported by the public. If successful, it provides an opportunity for officers to learn and improve to the point that they become productive, reliable and valued employees.

When discipline is non-existent or feeble it will result in the continuation of poor or bad behavior, it will undermine the authority of supervisors, it will demoralize those employees who do work hard and behave appropriately and ultimately, it will result in the deterioration of the public trust and confidence.

The same thing results when disciplinary process takes too long. It's difficult for fellow officers to understand and accept that co-workers who misbehave can receive suspensions at full pay that span months and years. Can anyone imagine how demoralizing it must be to see a suspended officer having unfettered time off to do whatever they wish, including hobbies, travel or even other employment, all while receiving the same pay as an officer working full time?

How must the public view that? This just cannot be allowed and every department should take a firm stance against it. In my opinion, an officer suspended with pay should be required to attend the office full time and be assigned duties appropriate to the officer and to the behavior that resulted in the suspension.

Certain behavior, especially criminal, is so detrimental to the effective operation of a police department that it justifies immediate and significant response. In many cases this type of behavior has attracted public and media attention and the very reputation of the entire department may rest in how it is handled in terms of speed and significance.

Where behavior is overtly and deliberately criminal in nature and absent powerful mitigating circumstances, an officer should be immediately terminated or at the very least be suspended without pay and then terminated at the first opportunity.

Honesty and integrity is an integral requirement for any police officer. If an officer's conduct has destroyed that, they may well have rendered themselves unsuitable for further employment in law enforcement.

If an officer's conduct is outrageous, evil, and inhumane or offends the standards of human conduct, immediate and severe action should be taken and must be seen to be taken. This might require an immediate suspension and if the act or behavior is proved to have occurred, an immediate escalation of discipline up to or including termination.

In my opinion, an employee who makes unauthorized, negative comments to the media or in the public about fellow officers or the police department should be immediately terminated! Such comments are almost impossible to counter, rebut or put into context and often leave the public with a very negative and unwarranted perception of the department and the individual officers. I simply cannot imagine private business tolerating that sort of behavior. I can say with absolute certainty that no employee of mine would ever see their desk again if they were to do something of that nature. No organization or police force should allow an employee to force them into "management by media."

In major incidents, when evidence is unambiguous, clear and beyond doubt, it's probably well worth the department taking immediate action to terminate or suspend the officer without pay. Should the employee feel unfairly treated, they have the option to seek resolution through the courts or other available process. If an organization has acted with cause, in a fair and reasonable manner, they should not fear a court challenge.

Many private companies and even other government organizations seem to be willing and able to immediately terminate an employee for cause and police departments should be no different. In fact, it could be argued that given the harm that can be done to the public and the department by a rogue officer, police departments should be most committed to this action when required. If a court or other independent body overturns a decision to terminate, at least the department cannot be faulted for failure to act.

I would think it advisable for every department to have some system in place that provides for a disciplinary record to follow the employee in the event they move or transfer. New supervisors should have access to that file to ensure they are able to monitor problem behavior and ensure that any remedial training, guidance or program has been completed or has been effective.

Certainly a discipline record might be a relevant factor when considering the employee's suitability for promotions and certain job functions. Individual departments would have to determine whether minor incidents should be expunged from that record after a certain amount of time had passed with no recurrence.

Departments should carefully consider their policies and procedures for providing the public with the specific details of the behavior that resulted in discipline. Most media outlets will give excessive amounts of coverage to police misconduct and many will attempt to put it in the worst and most embarrassing context possible. In my opinion, it should not be necessary to give them any more detail than is absolutely necessary. This would especially be true for personal issues such as domestic disputes, personal or sexual relationships and alcohol related actions.

It may well be sufficient to provide the press with the fact that an officer had been disciplined for conduct unbecoming or abuse of alcohol or a breach of ethics related to a personal relationship. In other words, keep details as generic as possible. This protects not only the department and the other officers, but also the offending officer and his family from public humiliation. In many cases the offending officer already faces a daunting challenge in correcting the aberrant behavior and rehabilitating his work and personal life without adding the public flogging that can result.

POLICE DISCIPLINE RESEARCH

In 2011 an excellent study regarding police discipline was conducted by Darrell W. Stephens. Stephens is a retired chief of police for the Charlotte-Mecklenburg Police Department. He is currently on the faculty of the Johns Hopkins University and is the executive director of the Major Cities Chiefs Association. It is not my intention to reiterate the entire report but he makes several interesting points which should be considered.

Intentional vs. Unintentional Errors

Employees will make errors that could be classified as intentional and unintentional.

An **unintentional** error is an action or decision that turns out to be wrong, but at the time it was taken, seemed to be in compliance with policy and the most appropriate course based on the information available. A supervisor, for example, might give permission for a vehicle pursuit to continue on the basis that the vehicle and occupants met the general description of one involved in an armed robbery. The pursuit ends in a serious accident, and it is learned the driver was fleeing because his driver's license was expired. Under these circumstances, the supervisor's decision would be supported because it was within the policy at the time it was made.

Unintentional errors also include those momentary lapses of judgment or acts of carelessness that result in minimal harm (backing a police cruiser into a pole for example, failing to turn in a report, etc). Employees will be held accountable for these errors but the consequences will be more corrective than punitive unless the same errors persist.

An **intentional** error is an action or a decision that an employee makes that is known to be in conflict with law, policy, procedures or rules (or should have [been] known) at the time it is taken. Generally, intentional errors will be treated more seriously and carry greater consequences.

Within the framework of intentional errors there are certain behaviors that are entirely inconsistent with the responsibilities of police employees. These include lying, theft, or physical abuse of citizens and other equally serious breaches of the trust placed in members of the policing profession. The nature of the police responsibility requires that police officers be trustworthy and truthful.

Any police department should terminate an employee's employment when it is clear the employee is intentionally engaging in an effort to be untruthful. Every effort should also be made to separate individuals from the department if they are found to have engaged in theft or serious physical abuse of citizens.

Processes generally take an excessive amount of time to complete.

In large departments, it takes about six months to complete a complaint investigation, reach a finding and determine the disciplinary action if the allegation is sustained. In the most serious cases this time can be increased significantly and, when discipline is appealed, it can take well over a year or longer to completely resolve the matter. An article in the *Atlanta Journal-Constitution* described a police officer who had been on administrative leave for four years for a criminal allegation before he was charged with a felony sexual assault. He was only one of 26 officers who had been placed on administrative leave for a long period of time pending case investigation (Torpy, 2009). The impact of discipline on the officer and the messages to the department and to the community are severely compromised the longer it takes from the time the misconduct occurred to its resolution.

Processes and outcomes often do not appear to be fair to employees.

Several factors contribute to the impression held by many employees that the disciplinary process is not fair. First, discipline is a personnel matter and in many states and cities, personnel issues are confidential. In these locations, departments cannot disclose the discipline or the circumstances that led to the decision. Second, there may be real or perceived variations in the punishment for similar offenses. Thirdly, the time period that has elapsed from the time the misconduct occurred to when the sanctions are imposed sometimes influences employees' opinions. This is especially true if an employee has corrected their behavior and produced good work in the meantime and then receives the actual sanction some time later.

Processes and outcomes may be influenced by the amount of publicity the alleged misconduct receives.

A high profile incident of officer misconduct may affect the investigation and the outcome of the discipline process. In some cases the process is expedited while others are slowed down considerably by all the attention. In a case in Portland, Ore., that received extensive news media attention, it took more than three years for the chief to reach a decision in an incident where a Taser was used and the person being arrested died. The chief determined the officer acted within policy but the officer was suspended because he did not send the victim to the hospital soon enough (Bernstein, 2009). In another case three years later, the same officer was placed on administrative leave for shooting a 12-year-old girl with a bean bag shotgun because she was resisting arrest. Union leaders claimed the suspension was more about the visibility of these cases than the behavior of the officer (Pitkin, 2009).

High-profile cases are particularly difficult for police executives and the community. The news media may disseminate information, video or photo images provided by citizens before the departmental hierarchy even knows something has happened. Executives then have to make statements as soon as possible with very limited information, and what they say may change (and often does) as the investigation gets under way and progresses. The community struggles with sorting out what happened as they hear conflicting statements or see segments of videotapes that include only part of the encounter with officers (Stephens, 2011).

9

POLICE IN THE JUSTICE SYSTEM

Military justice recognizes that a soldier's actions must be judged by others in the military. Can a police officer find justice in the public system?

When police officers commit intentional, premeditated criminal acts, there is rarely any defense that could be related to their duties as an officer. What can complicate the situation is when police officers are accused of or charged with actions committed during the execution of their duties.

It's complicated due to the very subjective nature of the many actions and decisions that an officer deals with. The confrontational and violent situations they are called to attend and the different options and degrees of force that may be available. In addition, they must make their decisions and carry out their actions while remaining not only within the narrow confines of the law, but also within all of the various departmental policies that may apply.

This raises a very critical question. Can a police officer involved in a serious, duty related incident, find a jury of their peers in the public domain? Can a police officer receive true justice in a Public justice system? To answer those questions, perhaps a comparison could be made to the Canadian and US military.

Long ago both governments recognized that actions and decisions taken in war and battle conditions could only be properly judged by others with similar experience. In answer, they created a separate system of justice for the military called the Uniform Code of Military Justice in the United States and the National Defense Act Code of Service Discipline in Canada. Military personnel are subject to this system and any discipline or charges which arise from their military duties are dealt with in a military court with a judge and jury composed of military personnel.

The military is well aware that acts, decisions and errors made in combat situations may appear to be completely foreign, negligent or even criminal to the public and that the only fair judgment would be from those with similar experiences and knowledge. As an example, the military knows several things are virtually guaranteed when soldiers go to war.

They know that there will be some casualties from "friendly fire" or human error incidents. They know that there will be unintentional collateral death and injury to civilians due to human error incidents. And they know that combat stress will have both involuntary and unpredictable effects on soldiers and may result in uncharacteristic and adverse behavior.

I discussed at some length in an earlier chapter some of the factors that can and do influence decisions, actions, judgments and memory of officers involved in critical incidents or combat stress incidents. Can an untrained and inexperienced public be expected to understand or empathize with that? Can even a prosecutor or a judge who has never personally experienced similar incidents truly appreciate and take into account those critical factors that might so clearly act as mitigating circumstances? Would education and training be enough? These are all very tough questions, especially with lives, careers and even personal freedom at risk

Not for a moment am I advocating that police officers should be excused for excessive use of force or for actions they take in critical or tactical situations. Professionals must always be accountable. But surely we should at least contemplate the fact that it is their duty to enter and face the type of violent, emotional, volatile and physical confrontations that very few other human beings are ever challenged with and that many factors influence the final outcome.

I do feel strongly that this entire field of study requires much more research and discussion. I also believe that police departments have a vested interest in having psychologists or other professionals who are trained to at least understand those factors and who could provide expert evidence in this regard.

CASE STUDY:
Public pressure influencing changes?

In late 2010, the Emergency Task Force and the Guns and Gangs Unit of the Toronto Police Department executed a high risk search warrant on a residence in relation to firearms and weapons offences. The suspects, two brothers, had criminal histories and had spent time in jail. During the raid one of the suspects was shot and killed.

An investigation was conducted by the Special Investigations Unit. This is an independent investigative unit tasked with investigating serious police-involved incidents. Because the matter is still before the courts, few actual details are available. We do know that the suspect received a gunshot wound to his back and that based on the SUI investigation and report, Crown prosecutors charged the officer with manslaughter.

There was the inevitable public and media frenzy. The dead male was Nigerian and thus there were accusations of police racism. Approximately two years after charging the officer with manslaughter, the Crown increased the charges to second degree murder.

The officer's lawyer and the police union were outraged, stating that the charge had been upgraded to murder in the absence of any new or additional evidence. The implication was that public pressure had played a role. They expressed concern that police officers working in the city had lost confidence in the process and that it could result in officers hesitating when making split second, tactical decisions. Union president Mike McCormack stated that the charge would have a long lasting and severe impact and that it was "tragic for our officers."

As discussed earlier, experts know and can explain how the delay from when an officer makes the decision to shoot to when the bullet strikes and the suspect's movements in the meantime, might result in wounds that can make it appear that the officer was not under threat when in fact they were. Can untrained civilians understand that?

CASE STUDY:
Criminal charges for policy breach?

In 2011, an RCMP constable with approximately two years of service attempted to stop a suspicious vehicle in the White Rock,

B.C. area. The vehicle fled and the officer began a pursuit. A short distance later the suspect vehicle collided with a parked car, then accelerated through a red light, striking and killing a pedestrian.

The Vancouver Police Department was called in to conduct the investigation. Once the investigation was completed, they forwarded the results to the Crown counsel. The Crown in turn laid charges of Dangerous Driving Causing Death — against the police officer!

There is no indication that the officer himself drove in a dangerous manner. He did not collide with any other vehicles or with the pedestrian and there was no evidence to suggest the officer forced the suspect vehicle off the road, or in any other way caused him to strike the pedestrian, other than by pursuing him.

While I can't say for certain, it is much more likely that the constable was found to have breached departmental vehicle pursuit policy than to have actually driven in a dangerous manner himself. If that was in fact the case, then it should be of great concern to every officer because the ramifications are broad based and significant.

Could an officer who is involved in a fully justified shooting be charged with murder if they were found to have used non-issue ammunition in breach of departmental policy? What about those cases where an officer feels they are within policy at the time they took action but an investigation after the fact determines they were not? Could they be charged *criminally* for what amounts to a breach of policy?

CASE STUDY:
A life-threatening struggle

In 2008, police in a medium sized US city were called to attend a disturbance involving two males who were arguing in the parking lot of an apartment building. Upon arrival they observed the two men shouting and pushing each other. When the officers intervened, one of the males became combative and began to push and shove one of the officers. When the second officer went to his assistance, the second male jumped on his back and pulled him to the ground. At this point both officers were engaged in a physical struggle and neither was able to disengage enough to access their batons or pepper spray. It quickly became clear that neither male was attempting to escape but rather were escalating the violence in an apparent attempt to injure the officers.

During the fight, one of the officers was able to get his arm around the suspect's neck and apply a chokehold, which seemed to be the only method available to him. When he felt the suspect cease struggling, he released the hold and the suspect slumped to the ground. He placed him in handcuffs and went to the assistance of the other officer. The second suspect was placed in hand cuffs and the officers turned their attention to the other male. It was at this point they discovered that he was not breathing. They immediately summoned an ambulance and began to attempt resuscitation. In spite of all efforts, the suspect died on route to the hospital. It was later determined that his larynx had been crushed and the suspect had suffocated.

An investigation was conducted by an independent investigative unit. It was determined that the officers had been assaulted and that they had no opportunity to use their batons or pepper spray. It was further determined that they were entitled to use force to protect themselves and to affect the arrest of the suspects. It was also noted that the police board for this particular police department had adopted a policy prohibiting the use of chokeholds by their officers.

Based on the breach of that policy, the investigative unit forwarded their report to the district attorney. The matter was reviewed and a charge of manslaughter was laid against the police officer.

This officer was ultimately acquitted, as he should have been, but the emotional and psychological trauma of the charge and subsequent trial had to have been incredible. Added to the already existing trauma caused by the taking of a human life, one can only guess at the effect it must have had on this officer and his family.

There can be little doubt that this charge was laid, not because the officer had used excessive or unnecessary force, but because he had breached the policy prohibiting choke holds. An officer, potentially in a fight for his life, had done what he felt he had to in order to survive and was charged criminally. How do we allow this sort of thing to happen?

―――――――

These types of incidents are always disturbing to me. Police officers are asked to perform certain duties, some of which hold the risk of unintended consequences and collateral damage. Then, in an effort to minimize that risk, we insist on encumbering those duties with numerous restrictions and policies. Since it's almost impossible to create a policy which is applicable to every scenario, the individual officer is required to interpret how it applies in each particular situation.

More often than not this interpretation must be made instantly and in high stress circumstances. Then, if things go wrong, there's the inevitable search for someone to blame. *An officer who has breached a policy or even a portion of that policy is an easy target.*

If society is not prepared to accept any form of collateral damage as a result of policing then the course is clear. Simply ban certain police actions. In the case of police pursuits, have the courage to simply ban them. If someone flees, let them go! In the case of police use of force, simply ban any use of force. If someone resists arrest, just let them go! That should ensure that nobody ever got hurt or killed as a result of police action. Simple, right?

Of course I'm being facetious. There is simply no way of prohibiting all of the police functions that could result in unintended consequences or collateral damage. If they are to carry out their duties, police may have to use force in some cases. They may have to engage in vehicle pursuits, arrest people and even use lethal force at times. And yes, there must be policies, regulations and procedures in place for certain actions. But what are the potential ramifications if police officers start getting criminally prosecuted for simply acting outside of policy?

One of the concerns is that police officers may become so risk averse that they will be tempted to ignore or avoid certain circumstances or refuse to take certain action that might result in them being charged. This of course, would have its own very serious unintended consequences and would significantly compromise public and officer security.

But who could blame an officer working in the White Rock area for avoiding any form of police pursuit after seeing what happened to their colleague? Might an officer be tempted to ignore the belligerent drunk rather than making an arrest and risking assault charges? What if that same drunk then goes home and kills his wife? What if officers simply refuse to execute high risk search warrants for fear of having to use lethal force? Or if an officer hesitates or refuses to use lethal force for fear of being charged and that inaction results in someone's death?

Please don't misunderstand. I'm not for a moment suggesting that these things are happening, should happen or ever will happen. I am concerned however, that excessive policies and restrictions which are not totally clear and concise, can require an officer to walk too close to the edge where one small misstep can have disastrous consequences.

As I have stated several times, I do believe that professionals must be accountable for their actions and decisions. However, is it fair to ask officers to carry out their duties, walk that fine line and then throw them to the courts if they are simply found to be outside of policy? *Should police officers in a domestic war zone be held to a higher standard than a soldier in a foreign war zone?*

One can only hope that the justice system will recognize these issues and provide some degree of latitude based on the entire situation and all mitigating factors. It must be said, however, that hope offers little comfort when careers and personal freedom are at stake.

10

POLICE CULTURE

Is there a "police culture" and if so, is it a bad thing?

Much has been made about "police culture." The media often seem to infer that it is somehow sinister, secretive, unhealthy or toxic and that it is exclusive or cult-like in nature. In actual fact, a "culture," when applied to an occupation or small group, simply refers to people who share generally common standards, behaviors, experiences, goals, objectives and attitudes.

Many organizations have their own culture. There is a sports culture, an academic culture, a horse culture and a media culture, to name a few. A professional athlete is a member of a very small, elite group and may deal with issues that can only be truly understood by another professional athlete. Only another professional news reporter may know and understand the challenges and issues that a colleague may face. The same is true of police officers.

Police officers do share many common beliefs and experiences. They work in a profession that generates much public comment and criticism, with little of the requisite knowledge or understanding, and this can result in officer's feeling somewhat isolated from the general public. Fellow officers understand many of the emotions, the frustrations, the fears and the demands associated with law enforcement.

Police officers deal with evil and corruption, pain and suffering, cruelty and oppression and over time, develop coping skills that often comport as black humor, callousness, indifference or a lack of emotion. This is a trait commonly shared by emergency room nurses and doctors, combat soldiers, paramedics and firefighters. In order to function and carry out their responsibilities, police officers learn to compartmentalize their personal feelings and emotions.

When the public observes an officer smiling while at a fatal accident, joking at a murder scene or otherwise appearing to be unaffected by human suffering, it may appear to them that police officers don't care, have no feelings and may even be callous or cruel.

If only they knew how an officer might appear resolute and stoic on the outside and be torn up inside. If only they knew how every death, every cruelty, every inhumanity left its mark. If only they knew the human price every police officer pays. But they don't and they can't. And it's not their fault.

Police officers and police departments have, in the past, remained very silent about the job they do. . .and the public often criticizes what they fail to understand. I know it's impossible to explain everything, to counter every criticism and rebut every false story, but perhaps it's something to consider. Can we do a better job in this area? Perhaps we can.

Yes, there is a police culture. Police officers often do prefer to socialize with other officers, with those they understand and who understand them. They may prefer to avoid social gatherings where they might be regaled with general or specific complaints about police, unhappiness over a ticket or some other disparaging comments directed at law enforcement.

But it's not sinister. It's not toxic, unhealthy or a cult. It's not even exclusive. . .to join, all you have to do is become a police officer!

11

THE POLICE ENVIRONMENT

*If humans are such "social" creatures,
why are we so bad at it?*

As you might imagine, police officers come in all sizes, genders, cultures, races and religions. They come with their own biases, perceptions, beliefs and understandings. They come with different personalities, skills, abilities and attitudes and just about all of the normal diversity one would expect to find amongst a large group of people.

How then can this mix of humans be managed so that all parties feel that they are an important part of the organization, treat each other with dignity and respect, adhere to the work and policy requirements of the police department and achieve their maximum potential? Well, sadly and in short, they can't!

In a perfect world perhaps, but that is not what we have, so organizations and people can only do their best. There are, however, some things that might reduce the frustration, anger, misunderstandings and misperceptions that almost always occur when large groups of people work or live together.

1. From the day they are hired, every officer should be made fully aware of all departmental policies regarding interpersonal relations and that every employee must be treated in a respectful and dignified manner. They

must fully understand what is expected of them in the workplace and in the execution of their duties and they must fully understand the consequences should they act outside of these policies.

2. All front line supervisors should fully understand their responsibilities and all departmental policies regarding disciplinary and internal complaint matters. They must understand that one of their primary roles is to develop, mentor, guide and teach their subordinates and that punishment should be a last resort wherever possible.

3. Every department should adopt a disciplinary and internal complaint process that can be applied fairly and which gives an employee an option to appeal decisions.

4. Every employee must understand and agree that internal disputes, discipline or complaints must be dealt with in a timely and professional manner using the internal process and that unauthorized statements in public or the media are unacceptable.

5. Senior level supervisors must ensure that internal complaints and discipline are dealt with in a timely manner, that policies are uniformly enforced and adhered to and that supervisors and employees clearly understand the reason and purpose of decisions that are made.

6. Senior management should ensure that all supervisors and employees know and understand that supervisors may have different management styles and personalities and that significant latitude would be granted in this regard so long as policy guidelines were adhered to and employees were treated with dignity and respect.

7. Whenever possible, discussions or meetings with employees and supervisors regarding discipline and internal complaints should be recorded for accuracy and to assist with appeals decisions.

8. When appropriate, mediation and informal resolutions which are acceptable to all parties should be a goal considered in any policy.

One of the many challenges for a police department is to convince all levels of employees' supervisors or management that they must "buy in" to the departmental policies, changes in policies or new policies, even if they disagree with them. It's much the same with many organizations. You can have meetings, disagreements, discussions and different opinions, but at the end of the day, when the final decision is made by the general, CEO, commissioner or owner, employees and management need to show a unified front and either get on board or disembark.

If an employee finds it impossible to accept, obey or implement those policies or changes, they should be honest and honorable enough to resign and move on. Anything less will simply result in a disgruntled, dysfunctional employee and have significant adverse consequences for both that employee and the organization.

In spite of any action taken by police departments, there will always be some internal conflict and it can range from minor, quickly resolved matters, to serious issues like bullying and sexual harassment.

Like with so many other things, no serious discussion can occur unless all parties are speaking the same language. In order to do that, there must be some agreement on the definitions and terminology being used, and on what sort of action is determined to fall within those definitions.

BULLYING OR SUPERVISION?

One of the very serious allegations leveled against many police departments and very recently against the RCMP has been that there is a culture of "bullying" and that management is either actively involved or ignores it. While there may well be some isolated cases of inappropriate bullying, I can honestly say that in my 21 years with the RCMP I was never bullied by anyone, I never bullied anyone and I never saw anything I would consider bullying. I think the crux of the matter is contained in my last comment.

I suspect that a person's perception of bullying depends upon what you consider bullying to be. In any police department, and the RCMP is no different, there have always been certain employees that required a higher level of supervision, counseling, guidance and discipline than others. I suspect that some of those officers feel that they are being unfairly picked on, harassed or bullied, but are they?

Should supervisors really stop supervising for fear that an employee might be offended? Should employees be allowed to produce shoddy work, act unprofessionally or even endanger other officers and the public because of concern that any criticism may result in their feeling harassed or bullied? I certainly hope not. That is not to suggest that an employee needs to be ridiculed or humiliated, but to some, even the most constructive criticism will be resented.

Because the safety of fellow officers and the public often depends upon the actions and decisions made by an officer, demands and expectations from both peers and supervisors can be quite high, mistakes bluntly pointed out and debriefings critical and often harsh by some standards. I will admit that this can be very difficult if you are thin-skinned or sensitive to criticism, but when the stakes are high and the effects of an error so major, I'm not sure there is room for a different approach.

Police departments are often accused of being too "military" in nature. Truthfully, that was not my experience. It must be said however, that there are many situations in police work where it would be inappropriate to call a meeting, form a committee, consider everyone's opinion, arrive at a consensus, and then put an action plan into place. Sometimes an order has to be followed immediately and to the letter or the consequences can be grave. Is that being too "military"?

When it comes to criticism, one could equate a police organization to a professional sports team where the poor play of any individual player may affect the entire team. I suspect that when the dressing room doors close, there is some blunt discussion about a players lack of performance, and it will be leveled by both players and coaching staff. In policing, the safety of fellow officers and the public depend upon the actions and decisions of individual officers and, like the team, expectations are high and criticism can be harsh and pointed.

Again, I suspect that some officers take exception to such criticism, believe it is directed at them because of personality, gender, race, culture or religion and have a very difficult time dealing with it. Instead of using it as a learning process, they allow it to cause resentment. Over time this resentment may evolve into a firm conviction that he/she has been unfairly treated or bullied...but that doesn't make it so.

Some of the best bosses and colleagues that I ever worked with were tough, no-nonsense police officers who told it the way it was and left you with no doubt about where you stood with them. It is simply a fact that different supervisors will have different personalities and management styles. Some may be friendly, open and diplomatic. Some may be gruff, closed-off and blunt. Some may be more or less tolerant about certain issues than others. Some will be good, strong effective leaders and some will not. I always felt that it was the subordinate's responsibility to adapt to a supervisor's style and not the other way around.

Having said that, there were times when I felt it necessary to speak frankly with a supervisor and in those cases I found that, when appropriate, I had every opportunity to speak, be heard, argue and discuss most issues and concerns with supervisors including those at senior levels. Certainly, common sense had to be used. The conversation had to be professional, respectful and as importantly, in private, but I was given the opportunity to convey my position. Sometimes it resolved the issue or resulted in the supervisor amending their behavior or decision and sometimes not. But as the old saying goes, "sometimes the boss is a fool, sometimes the boss is wrong...but the boss is always the boss!"

CASE STUDY:
Standing up respectfully

Shortly after my transfer to Surrey detachment, a position opened up on the Major Crime Section. This was a position I coveted and felt qualified for so I put my name forth as a candidate. I was of course disappointed when I was informed that the Inspector would not approve my selection. I was told the reason for his decision was that he felt it was not fair to the officers who had been stationed at Surrey for years when I had only been there a short period of time. I asked for and was granted a meeting with him.

Now, remember that this was in 1985 and the RCMP was certainly more paramilitary in nature than it is today. I met with the Inspector in his office and advised him, with respect and in a professional manner, that I would like an opportunity to express my own thoughts about the matter. He agreed.

I first stressed how the RCMP had always made clear the importance of mobility and transferring of members and that Surrey was my fourth posting. I pointed out that I had spent four years in a northern posting and had gained significant experience in plain clothes duties and major crime investigations. I concluded by stating that while I did understand his wanting to reward long time Surrey members, excluding my name would in effect be punishing me because I had done what the force had asked and accepted numerous transfers.

I can tell you that I did *not* have high hopes. In those days it was rare for an officer to reverse a ruling. In fact, it was rather rare that, as a constable, I'd even been granted a meeting. That's why I will never forget when he told me that he had been swayed by my argument and the manner in which I had presented it and agreed to allow my name to go forward. I did subsequently get the position based on experience and qualifications.

There are several points to this story. Instead of receiving the Inspector's decision and becoming disgruntled, I was proactive. In being proactive, I was given a fair opportunity to express my thoughts and opinions. I did so professionally, maturely and respectfully. The result was that I achieved my goal.

Would I have been disappointed if I'd not been granted a meeting, or if the Inspector had refused to change his position? Certainly I would have. Perhaps I'd even have felt angry and unfairly dealt with. But at that point I would've had to make a choice. Do I define my career with bitterness and resentment, thus ensuring that I will never achieve my goal? Or do I get back to work and wait for the next opportunity, knowing that my goal has only been delayed?

CASE STUDY:
Learning from mistakes

While on the Serious Crimes Section at Surrey, we were tasked with an investigation into a police involved shooting. Two uniform officers had responded to a complaint of a male, armed with a knife, threatening residents in a trailer park. Based on the officer's statements and witness accounts, the following circumstances were determined.

Upon arrival the officers were directed to the suspect's trailer and found him inside. He had been drinking and had a large butcher knife in his hand. As the officers approached, the suspect came to the doorway and the officers engaged him in conversation. He began to calm down but refused to put the knife down or to move outside of the trailer. As the conversation continued, the suspect moved away from the doorway and back into the living area. At this point one of the officers entered the trailer in an effort to continue talking with the suspect. The second officer remained just outside the doorway but still able to see inside.

In spite of efforts to calm the suspect, he began to become agitated again and moved towards the officer in a threatening manner. The second officer, who had his weapon drawn, ordered the suspect to drop the knife and he refused. When he again moved in a threatening manner, this officer fired. The suspect dropped to the floor, seriously but not fatally wounded.

The investigation determined that the shooting was justified and in fact it had been. Both officers had to be commended for their personal courage and their serious efforts to engage the suspect verbally in an effort to calm him and resolve the incident without use of force.

What the investigation also determined was that a young and inexperienced officer had made a tactical error when he entered the trailer. He had put himself into a position of danger by being too close to an armed suspect with no viable escape route. When the suspect began to threaten him, he had no place to retreat, which in turn forced the second officer to resort to lethal force.

When we held the incident debriefing, this officer's tactical error was pointed out to him in a clear and straightforward manner. To his credit, this was a mature and professional officer and he accepted the criticism as it was meant, constructively and as a learning experience. This young officer could have chosen to be upset, disgruntled or feel bullied but he did not. What he did do was go on to become one of the best officers I had seen or worked with and was a credit to the force.

I have, on several occasions, mentioned the importance of context and perspective. In discussing workplace bullying and employee discontent within police departments, the same thing applies. The following research data reveals that many organizations face the same challenges and that many employees feel underappreciated, bullied or harassed.

RESEARCH

Bad Bosses the Reason for Unhappiness

In 2012, workplace psychology specialist Michelle McQuaid conducted a study that revealed that 65% of Americans would choose a new boss over a pay raise (McQuaid, 2012). The report went on to state that in the US it's costing businesses approximately $360 billion per year in lost productivity and that employees feel unappreciated, uninspired, lonely and miserable.

The study found that only 36% of Americans are happy at their jobs, 65% blame their boss for their unhappiness and 60% said they would do a better job if they got along better with their boss.

The study was remarkably silent about why the 65% didn't start their own business, how their own performance was rated or why they did not seek another job. . .Hmmm?

On the Job Bullying

In 2011, a 5,671 person survey by CareerBuilder found that the eldest and youngest employees were at the greatest risk of being bullied. According to this survey, three out of 10 employees 55 and older or 24 and younger reported having been bullied at work. The most common forms of workplace bullying were exclusion, sabotage, verbal hostility and physical intimidation.

Loraleigh Keashly, an associate professor at Wayne State University, goes on to state that for it to be considered bullying or harassment, the behavior must form a pattern over time and not simply be isolated incidents.

This is a very important and critical statement. In fact it bears repeating. *The behavior must form a pattern over time and not simply be isolated incidents.*

CASE STUDY:
Toxic relationships

Upon my promotion to sergeant at Surrey Detachment, I was responsible for the supervision of three corporals, approximately 20 constables and five unionized municipal employees. The five municipal employees were all female administrative staff and it quickly became clear that I had inherited a serious workplace conflict.

All five were excellent workers but two of them had a very bitter almost hateful relationship and it was beginning to affect productivity and moral. I called a general meeting and made it quite clear that I expected everyone to act professionally and to treat each other with respect. For a few days everything calmed down.

Then one day one of the employees, I'll call her Jane, came to my office and reported that she had been verbally abused by the other who I will call Sue. I met with the other employees and it was evident that Sue had been the aggressor. I spoke with her independently and advised her that if this behavior continued, I would have to take disciplinary action. She was upset but went back to work. A few days later I walked into their work space and asked one of the staff to type some work I required. Sue, who I had just counseled, became upset and told her not to do the work as she felt Jane was not pulling her weight. Since I knew for a certainty that Jane did more than her share of the work, I immediately asked Sue to come to my office. I advised her that she had not only countermanded a request I had made, she had been openly disrespectful to the other employees. With that, I gave her a written reprimand.

The next day she didn't show up for work. As she had not called in sick, I contacted her at home and was told that she would not be back to work as she was taking stress leave. As per policy, I asked her to provide the written recommendation from her doctor once she had it and left it at that. The next thirty days were actually quiet and peace reigned in the office. The four remaining staff were much happier and more productive and advised that they would prefer that it remained just the four of them.

After approximately 30 days, Sue returned to work and the tension level soared. For the first few days things went smoothly. Then I overheard Sue make a very disparaging comment to Jane again. At that point my patience expired and I brought Sue into my office, provided her with a second written warning and advised her that I would be taking steps to transfer her to a different unit within the detachment. I explained that she was a good worker and I was not trying to have her fired, but that her relationship with Jane was so toxic that she seemed unable to control herself and in fact was the aggressor. She was very upset and left the office again.

The next day, the detachment commander notified me that Sue's union had lodged a complaint against me and wanted to have a meeting. A few days later the union officials, the Detachment Commander and I met to discuss the matter. In spite of the fact that they represented both employees and that we were not attempting to have Sue fired, the union was very adamant that she was being mistreated and should not be transferred. Nothing we said seemed to sway them. Finally I told them that the relationship between the two was so virulent that it was not beyond the possibility of one of them committing a violent act against the other or possibly to themselves and that I wanted it clearly on the record that I had identified that as a legitimate concern.

One day later Sue was moved from my unit to another. Over the course of the next few days, all four municipal staff and a number of RCMP members stopped by my office to thank me for taking action. Even I had not realized just how deeply this one toxic relationship had affected everyone in the office.

There is no question that Sue was unhappy with my actions and the result. I'm sure she genuinely feels picked upon or bullied and has no doubt told many others that very thing. But those of us who worked with or near her and observed the behavior would tell a very different story.

———

As has been mentioned earlier, police department personnel reflect the demographics and characteristics of the society and the generation from which they are hired. Education systems and sports organizations seem to be moving to a "nobody fails, nobody loses, everybody wins, everybody passes" approach and adults are taught that any criticism directed towards a young person will damage their self esteem.

It makes one question if we are in danger of creating a generation that has little experience with criticism, constructive or otherwise. Will this result in employees who may overreact, or take too personally, even mild criticism or disapproval, to the point that they genuinely confuse supervision with bullying? There's a study for another day!

12

SEXUAL HARASSMENT AND GENDER BIAS

*I've often wondered...what advice would I give
my daughter if she were to join the RCMP?*

One of the most devastating allegations that can be levied
against a police department is one of internal sexual harassment. In fact, it is so serious that I have dedicated an entire
chapter to the topic.

As with bullying, it is important to start a discussion about
sexual harassment with a definition. For example, what con-
stitutes sexual harassment as opposed to gender bias? While
I admit these are my own definitions, they do closely follow
the same parameters as several other government or corporate
definitions.

Sexual Harassment:
- When a supervisor utilizes their position to coerce sexual
  cooperation through the use of threats or promises.

- When a supervisor utilizes their position to punish or
  reward a subordinate based on sexual cooperation.

- When colleagues use sexually-based touching, comments
  or actions that might reasonably be expected to make
  another colleague uncomfortable, humiliated or
  embarrassed.

Gender Bias:
- When any employee or employees are treated differently, unequally or unfairly, be it better or worse, based on their gender.

SEXUAL HARASSMENT

Sexual Harassment, as described above, has occurred in various workplaces for years. In my opinion it was not okay a hundred years ago and it will not be okay a hundred years from now. It is simply unacceptable on many levels and in those cases where it can be proven to have occurred, the offending party must at least be considered for significant discipline. Having said that, I also believe that, while it may have been more prevalent years ago, it is much rarer today.

Quite recently, approximately 300 female RCMP officers, most of them retired, launched a large, class action law suit claiming sexual harassment going back as far as 1974. At this time the case has not been to court and all of the allegations are so far unsubstantiated. Furthermore, since no actual details have been released it is not known what claims were actual sexual harassment as opposed to gender bias as opposed to totally unfounded.

The point should also be made that these types of historical complaints relating to human behavior require that the actions from approximately 40 years ago be judged using the standards of today. This is a precarious situation and could well set dangerous precedents. For example, society's attitude on gay rights was much different 40 years ago.

Attitudes towards crime, drinking, smoking, recreational

drug use, education, discipline and many other social mores have changed significantly in the past 40 years. Many of those changes have been for the better but is it reasonable or appropriate to judge the actions of people from one generation or era using the social standards of today?

Because it was reported in the media, these allegations were broadcast widely and received much public comment. In fact, if one were to believe the media reports, you would think that sexual harassment was running rampant through the force, that the men were all misogynistic bullies and the women all weak, dominated victims unable or unwilling to stand up for themselves.

Well, that was certainly *not* the force I recall. Virtually all of the female members I worked with were strong and confident women who simply would not tolerate sexual harassment.

Again, while even one case of sexual harassment is bad, putting things into context is important. So, even if one assumed that all 300 allegations were legitimate sexual harassment complaints, which is highly unlikely, it's a very small number compared to the thousands of female officers, serving and retired, who have been members of the RCMP since 1974. I know that there are those who have and will make the argument that if there are 300 females who will report it there must, by definition, be hundreds more who are victims but who have not reported it. This is a spurious argument and one which could be made about any company or organization in the world. One could just as easily say that if a particular company or organization had received no complaints about sexual harassment, it was only because it had not been reported. It seems unfair, inaccurate and inherently wrong to simply make that sort of general assumption and it is certainly inappropriate to make those types of unsupported statements in the media.

I have publicly stated on three radio talk shows that I had never, in 21 years in the RCMP, personally seen or even heard of a case of sexual harassment as described in the previous definition. That is not to say it has never occurred. I suspect it has. What I do question is the frequency and in some cases, the circumstances.

I have, over the years, however, seen and heard many things that, judged by today's standards, could be deemed inappropriate. And it has come from *both* males and females. I have seen and heard sexual bantering from both males and females which, in my opinion, was given and received with humor and certainly never crossed into abusive or oppressive behavior. I have seen fraternization between male and female members. At times that lead to hurt feelings and anger but again, to my way of thinking, this is not sexual harassment. I have seen members meet, date and be married happily for years. I have also seen Members meet, date, and have a very acrimonious split. I have seen spurned and unhappy males and females. I have seen mutually accepted flirting and I've seen some flirting from both genders that was unwelcome.

When you put males and females into a workplace, it's naive to think that a certain amount of sexually based interaction won't occur. In fact, many social gatherings involving males and females provide ample evidence that sexually based innuendo and flirting is not the sole domain of either gender. At what point does any of this cross the line and become sexual harassment? I don't really know. Based on the earlier study by Loraleigh Keashly, there would have to be some consistency or pattern over time and not just random or isolated incidents, for it to be considered genuine harassment.

I do think, that on occasion, flirting or bantering which was mutually acceptable between two or more colleagues, may suddenly be used as an accusation of sexual harassment if one of those colleagues suddenly becomes unhappy for some other, completely unrelated reason. For example, a male and female may each engage in mutually acceptable flirting, conversations or even actions, with neither feeling it was inappropriate. Then, perhaps one of them ends that relationship. Perhaps one receives discipline for some, unrelated issue, is denied a job position or promotion or anything else than might cause them to feel angry or mistreated. They may be angry with that specific colleague or maybe with the entire department. Whatever the case, they decide after the fact that the sexually-based activity was not mutual and constituted sexual harassment. The same sort of thing occurs in divorce proceedings all the time. One spouse suddenly comes up with all sorts of accusations and complaints about the other that had never been an issue during the marriage.

When it comes to sexual harassment, even if you were to discard my own experience, there are some things that are difficult to explain and a few common sense factors that shouldn't be ignored.

First, if sexual harassment was occurring in anything other than very isolated cases, it's hard to imagine that I would not have at least "heard" a female officer complain or make mention of it. To this date, in spite of having many female friends and associates in the force, I have still never heard of a single such incident or even a third-party incident.

Second, there are many male and female members in the force who are married to each other, some quite senior in rank, and it is difficult to imagine that they would tolerate sexual harassment if they saw or were aware of it.

Third, there are many senior members who now have daughters serving in the force. Surely a daughter would not fear reporting this to a parent and I find it very difficult to believe that any senior officer whose own daughter was a victim of, or witness to, sexual harassment, would tolerate or condone it.

Fourth, there are and have been many very senior female commissioned officers in the Force, including Deputy Commissioner Bev Busson, who was the commanding officer of E Division and for a time, the acting commissioner of the RCMP. Is it realistic to believe that they would simply ignore genuine sexual harassment if they were aware of it or if it was reported to them?

So this begs the question. When did this harassment occur? Where did it occur? Who was involved? Was it reported to management? If not, why not? If yes, was any action taken? What was the result of that action? These are all questions that are currently unanswered and until they are, the stigma that these unverified allegations have left on the reputation of the Force will continue to be destructive and demoralizing.

An allegation of sexual harassment is an easy one to make, in that the media simply loves these types of stories, and is more than willing to broadcast them. It's also a very difficult one to defend against. If the employer goes public in a defensive move, they are branded as bullies and having a "toxic culture." Remaining silent simply reinforces the allegations.

As with the bullying accusations, this is simply another example of why police departments and all officers should be so adamantly opposed to employees making unsubstantiated allegations in the media. It just does not allow for any context, verification or rebuttal. It disregards the "other side of the story" and leaves the public with an extremely negative and possibly erroneous perception. The point I'm making is this: An employee who has an internal complaint must be required to make that complaint known to management in a timely manner and management must be allowed to conduct the internal investigation.

At the end of the day, every adult is responsible for setting and indicating the standards of behavior that they will or will not accept from others. In essence, we must teach others how we will and will not be treated. Overreaction or under-reaction each have negative consequences and will certainly result in how we experience the workplace and how we interact with supervisors and colleagues. So, what are the options for an employee who is being sexually harassed? Well, I believe that reasonable options might be as follows:

1. Have a private and frank discussion with the offending supervisor or colleague. Make it absolutely clear that you did not appreciate the behavior and expect it to stop immediately. I suspect that if this step is taken in a timely and proper manner, it would result in an immediate end to the behavior in *most* cases.

2. If you are meeting with a supervisor and aren't comfortable meeting alone, you might consider having another more senior officer or a division or union representative present with you, although this would tend to make it more formal than might be desirable for a first meeting.

3. If the behavior were to continue and involved comments, gestures or inappropriate items or pictures, consider taking photographs or recordings to support your position and then make a formal complaint to a supervisor who is above the level of the offender. Make it clear that you attempted to resolve the matter informally and now expected action to be taken. Also state that you want to be informed of what action is taken.

4. If the behavior continues and involves touching, make a formal complaint to another supervisor above the level of the offender and make it clear to that supervisor that while you sincerely hope to avoid doing so, you are prepared to formally arrest and charge the offender if it happens again. Ask that action be taken and that you be informed of what that action was.

5. If the offender is a supervisor or senior officer, insist that they not be involved in any future evaluations or career decisions that would affect you.

6. If no action is taken in response to the complaint, take it to a higher level until action is taken. If you have attempted to resolve the matter informally without success, you *must* follow through until the matter is properly dealt with.

7. If a matter is officially dealt with, accept that it has been, even if you don't agree with the action taken or feel it was not severe enough. The goal is to have the behavior stop, not to seek revenge. If it doesn't stop, that is another issue and you will probably be required to take additional action.

8. If no level of supervisor or management will support your position, carefully review your position! Seriously, take an objective look at what you are complaining about. Discuss it with someone who can give you a neutral, objective opinion. If you still feel you have been a victim of sexual harassment and that nobody in the department will take it seriously, then you may have to seek outside legal counsel.

Once again, I ask not to be misunderstood. I have clearly stated that cases of legitimate sexual harassment are serious and must not be tolerated under any circumstances. There is no question that there have been, are and will be incidents of genuine sexual harassment and nothing I have written is meant to minimize the gravity of those cases.

We must, however, investigate each allegation fairly and impartially, and not be too quick to simply assume that if the allegation has been made it *must* be true.

GENDER BIAS

Gender bias exists in virtually every relationship involving men and women. Anyone who has been married or who has brothers and sisters or sons and daughters, knows that men and women process information differently. They perceive many situations differently, socialize differently and are, well. . .just different! These differences often form the basis for much stereotypical humor at the expense of men and women and there's nothing wrong with that.

One of the more popular books on the matter was John Gray's *Men are from Mars and Women from Venus*. It simply explained and poked fun at both genders and was so funny because it was so true. I've been married for many years; have a daughter, a daughter-in-law and four granddaughters. I love all of them to death, think they are absolutely amazing. . .but don't understand a single one of them!

Gender bias has many forms. From the minor, common sense and practical, to the major, patently unfair biases which adversely affects quality of life, careers and relationships. Certainly, gender bias can be a very serious issue requiring a significant and decisive response.

But all parties should be very careful to avoid describing acts of gender bias, regardless of seriousness, as sexual harassment, as the two are very different and have very different connotations.

In many offices and work places, men and women have engaged in various forms of gender bias on a daily basis, often without even recognizing it as such. Truly, many incidents of gender bias simply reflect the different interests, skills, physical strengths, or other factors that are often practical, common sense methods for determining division of labor and which are not offensive to anyone.

For example, one might well find an office where the women organize the company Christmas party and the men organize the company golf tournament. Or perhaps the women maintain the coffee and lunch room supplies and the men are the ones who move furniture or heavy boxes of supplies. There are many similar examples I'm sure, and so long as nobody feels they are unfairly treated, there is rarely an issue.

Problems exist when a male or a female begins to feel that they are being treated unfairly based on their gender. In some cases there is a clear, easily measured bias. For example, if a supervisor called a duty related unit or section meeting and invited only male or only female officers, that would be a clear case of gender bias. If a department discouraged or refused to allow one specific gender to apply for internal job postings, this too would be clear and easily determined.

If a supervisor were to assign soft, non-dangerous type calls to female officers and the higher risk, dangerous calls to the male officers, this would be gender bias that would negatively impact both males and females. In situations like these, it would be incumbent on management to take action to rectify the situation immediately and take steps to ensure it did not occur again.

There are, however, other incidents of gender bias that are less easily identified and dealt with. For example, are all genders equally or proportionately represented in all job functions in a department and is that even always practical? Female officers may be highly desirable in child sexual assault units and this may have more to do with the victim's trust and response to different genders than it does to respective abilities between males and females.

A SWAT or riot team may be over-represented by male officers and this may have more to do with things like interests, physical size or aptitude than any real or intentional gender bias. In other words, are there occasions where there are practical and operational requirements which do and should determine personnel decisions, in spite of the fact that it treads on the edge of gender bias?

Another consideration when discussing gender bias involves pregnancy and maternity leave. There is no doubt this poses difficult questions and even more difficult solutions when departments attempt to select candidates for promotions or job positions based on qualifications that might include job experience. For example, there might be two candidates, one female and one male, who each have 7 years of service based on when they joined. Say the female officer had two children since she joined. This means that in all likelihood she would have spent approximately 1 year on light or reduced duty while pregnant and approximately 2 years on maternity leave. If the male had not taken an equal amount of time off for paternity leave or any other reason, there is a disparity in actual and genuine experience with the female having 4 years and the male having 7 years.

One can see the dilemma. Certainly no female should be punished for bearing children and that just can't be argued. On the other hand, a male officer may well have a legitimate argument that he was the more qualified, based strictly on genuine job experience. Naturally, a police department should want for two things in this case. That all employees are treated fairly and equitably and that the best candidate receives the promotion or job. The law seems quite clear that an employee cannot be discriminated against for taking maternity leave and it deals with many of the issues that might arise, but is very silent on the issue of lost job experience and its impact on future considerations. As with many such issues, there are bound to be any number of differing opinions and I'm not sure there is a perfect solution. If there is, I certainly don't have it!

Perception and interpretation becomes a huge factor in dealing with gender bias issues. For example, if a female officer gets a particular job or promotion there may be some male officers who will feel that it was based on her gender as opposed to her qualifications. Conversely, if a male officer received the same job or promotion, some female officers might feel they were passed over because of their gender.

Sadly, it seems to be a fairly common human trait amongst all genders that makes it difficult for people to have the personal insight, honesty and evaluation necessary to analyze situations factually, logically and dispassionately.

In many situations, doing so would reveal self-truths that are difficult to face. That perhaps another was more qualified, that your own work history was subpar or that maybe the criticism was legitimate and deserved. It's much easier to blame failure, disappointment and place criticism on someone or something other than ourselves. To deceive ourselves into believing it was because the supervisor or the police department was prejudiced, biased or sexist—in short, that it had nothing to do with our own shortcomings, lack of qualifications, poor attitude, or work history.

It has already been mentioned that women and men often process the same information much differently, and quite naturally this too can lead to misunderstandings, hurt and anger. A male supervisor may say exactly the same thing to a female officer that he has just said to a male officer and have it taken very differently. For example, a supervisor might make an offhand, casual comment to a male officer about their weight or deportment and because men are socialized differently, this may have little or no impact on "Joe" other than as a light, informal warning to watch his weight or personal grooming.

The very same comment directed in exactly the same manner might well be received much differently if the officer in question is named "Jane." Most women are simply more conscious and sensitive about physical appearance than most men. They will be more apt to take such a comment as a personal attack, as bullying or sexism. I know that in *my* house, such a comment would be best made from a considerable distance!

In actual fact, in most organizations, such comments would be totally unacceptable and indefensible. There are, however, some occupations like modeling, fashion or dancing where it might be a necessary and accepted part of supervision. Police work would fall somewhere in the "between" category, in that an officer's weight and personal grooming might well be a valid work issue depending upon the specific job requirement of the individual officer. Certainly an officer on the SWAT team might be expected to have a higher level of physical fitness than an officer on the Fraud Unit and a uniform patrol officer might have different standards than an officer in a more administrative type duty.

In the above example, personal appearance was used to make a point, but there are many other areas where men and women may have different values, attitudes and perceptions. Men tend to be more accustomed to rough humor, conversation and interaction and are generally less apt to take personal offence at being called by their last name, being teased or spoken to roughly, bluntly or critically. In fact I think it can be said that men are generally less sensitive to the actions and comments of others and often interact more casually.

Women, on the other hand, may tend to be much more sensitive to the actions and comments of others and are apt to take those things more personally. Even many women will tell you that interpersonal relationships between other women in a female-dominated workplace can be challenging and difficult. Conversely, many women are more socially considerate and empathetic than most men and it's this very trait that can make them such valued employees and supervisors. A female supervisor may be much more in tune with subordinates, be much kinder with criticism and make more effort to reach a consensus.

How then do organizations respond to this? Again, I think it goes back to treating all parties fairly, with dignity and respect. To be prepared to explain and justify decisions that are made, to be intolerant of gender bias and to avoid *at all costs* the hiring or promoting of officers based on any agenda, quota or affirmative action policy that is in itself gender biased.

I've often wondered what advice I would give my own daughter if she were to join the RCMP. I think I would tell her something like this:

You are now an adult. Your world is no longer one of playgrounds, classrooms or children. It is no longer one where awards are given for simply trying or showing up, where everyone gets a turn, where nobody fails, nobody loses and nobody gets criticized.

You are now a professional police officer. Your world now requires much of you. You must be strong yet remain flexible. You must stand up for yourself and others. Be true and honest to yourself. Be loyal to your colleagues and your department. Challenge unfair, biased or sexist decisions or actions, but understand that life isn't always fair. And always remember that you are part of a team, and that while you may not always like or get along with individual team-mates, it is still your team!

And finally, I would tell her:

Never be ashamed of being human. . .be ashamed if you act inhumanely.

Never be ashamed because a colleague acts unprofessionally. . .be ashamed if you do.

Never be ashamed of failing. . .be ashamed of not trying your best.

RESEARCH INTO RCMP HARASSMENT

In 2012, in response to several complaints and a class action lawsuit, the RCMP conducted a survey of approximately 426 female officers (RCMP, 2012). A number of responses indicated that female officers who had been bullied, harassed or mistreated had not reported the abuse to anyone for fear that they would be punished and the abuser would face no sanctions at all.

At the same time, the report revealed a widespread belief

within the force that such complaints, and the media coverage of them, have been exaggerated and blown out of proportion. Indeed, the report notes statistics related to complaints don't show significant numbers of harassment cases. It does, however, go on to suggest that this discrepancy may be due to the fact that women aren't reporting abuse when it happens: *"The result is a significant failure to report incidents and an unwillingness to discuss the issues with supervisors or management"* (RCMP 2012).

To my mind, this report creates a dilemma. How can an organization be expected to stop abuse if it is not being reported to them? Is it not being reported because of past failures to address the issues or have employees simply assumed that nothing would be done? How can a professional police officer, whose duty is to protect the public, be afraid to confront and report abuse happening to themselves or colleagues? It does create legitimate questions and concerns.

While I certainly have no personal expertise with this type of study, I do wonder at the validity of a question that allows a non response that simply says *"I was afraid to report abuse."* If it's a functional questionnaire and is intended to fully explore the issue, what it really needs to ask is:

- Who specifically were you afraid to report it to?
- Was your fear based on personal experience or knowledge?
- If so, what were the details of the incident that resulted in that experience or knowledge?
- If not based on personal experience or knowledge, what is it based on?

At least with those questions, the employee is required to give some specific response, which in turn might well be informative and constructive. A response that is too non specific offers little value. For example, if a survey questionnaire asks employees if they are happy in their work and they responded *"No, we don't trust management"* or *"No, we're intimidated by management"* and simply left it there, of what real value is that?

It makes it far too easy for any employee who happens to be unhappy for any reason or perhaps is only unhappy at the very moment they answer the survey, to simply answer any way they wish without the responsibility of providing any supporting evidence or information.

It's really no more valid than if an employer simply told an employee that they were not satisfied with their work and left it at that.

It provides no specific feedback and the employee can't really be expected to benefit from it or improve in any way.

This is why anonymous complaints and comments are generally considered unreliable unless supported with some other information.

13

STRESS LEAVE — USE AND ABUSE

Is there any employee benefit more abused than this?

I wonder if any one factor has so undermined the ability of an organization to manage employees as what's commonly referred to as "stress leave"? It's gotten to the point that if a supervisor does admonish or discipline an employee, no matter how warranted, that employee may well go on almost indefinite leave by claiming that their work environment is too stressful. Perhaps the new catch word is "toxic."

Stress leave has been so abused and misused that many officers refer to it, somewhat derisively, as "Time Off — Mad" or "P O' Leave." Now, a supervisor may be tempted to overlook certain deficiencies or behavior in an employee rather than risk losing them for several months or even years and that has a serious, long term negative effect on any organization.

I don't think anyone is unsympathetic to an officer who has genuinely gone through an extraordinarily traumatic experience — work, health or family wise. Every resource and means of assistance should be offered to these officers with the ultimate goal being a return to mental and emotional well being and a normal, productive life. Even so, there must be some reasonable time frame involved and if an employee is unable or unwilling to respond to treatment, some other action has to be contemplated.

Unfortunately, there are other officers who have no specific incident or cause, but who merely feel that their job "stresses" them out. If these incidents are examined closely, it would reveal that in many cases these officers are simply unhappy or disgruntled about something or with someone. It could be their job assignment, their supervisor, their co-workers or their department. They may have received a reprimand or discipline and feel they were treated poorly or unfairly, but the facts often show otherwise. They may have lost a grievance or a job opportunity, not because the process was unfair, but because they were wrong or unqualified or perhaps the other candidate was simply more qualified. That is life in virtually every workplace!

In those cases where an employee has a genuine complaint, they should be entitled to stand up for themselves and take appropriate action. This might include confronting another party or entering a complaint, grievance or appeal. That is how a professional deals with things, not by abandoning their job and colleagues and abusing stress leave.

In many other cases the employee does not have a genuine complaint and is simply disgruntled. In actual fact, there is no shortage of things that an employee might chose to be upset about in any large organization. They can be rather impersonal. The CEO, general or commissioner might not know your name or remember your birthday. Supervisors may not have or take the time to understand, mollify or cater to employees. They may actually be more concerned with getting the job done than making a particular employee happy. But hurt feelings, anger or wounded pride is not a valid reason to go on an extended stress leave. That is an abuse of the system and a theft of time.

I don't deny that police work, like many other occupations, can be stressful. Certainly not everyone is emotionally or physically suited to the job. That doesn't in any way make that person inferior or flawed. The individual just may not be suited to police work. When this occurs, is it not for a person's own benefit, as well as the organization's, to have that quickly determined so that both can move on?

From an administrative and operational view, how long can or should an employee be absent from work at full salary before they are deemed unfit or unsuitable for duty? It makes it almost impossible to manage resources, it places an unfair burden or stress on other officers and it costs the tax payer an enormous amount in wages as well as medical and psychological services.

In BC, there is an officer who has sued the police department for sexual harassment. This officer has been off work on stress leave since 2007 at full pay. Surely there is some job function this officer could do. If not, and if this person doesn't have the personal honor or integrity to resign and continue the legal battle on their own time, surely the department should move to terminate this person. This officer has now received approximately $450,000 in wages alone, to say nothing of the associated benefits and medical costs.

It's demoralizing to all honest, hard-working officers, to see colleagues abuse stress leave, often for months and even years. They not only see them abusing it, but also that they are seemingly allowed to do so without consequences. It's difficult to explain why their colleague is golfing, fishing or travelling on full pay while they remain behind to handle the extra burden.

An employee who wants to take stress leave should be required to provide significant evidence in the absence of some definitive traumatic incident. This should be especially true in those cases where an employee goes on stress leave shortly after any workplace event that might be expected to cause a normal degree of disappointment, resentment or anger but not debilitating stress. This would include losing out on a position or promotion, receiving a reprimand or discipline, losing a grievance, having an argument with a supervisor or colleague or any other normal or minor workplace conflict that can arise from time to time with any employee.

Surely an employee shouldn't simply be able to show a doctor's note and go on stress leave for years. Perhaps they should be required to obtain the professional opinion from a minimum of two psychiatric professionals, at least one of whom is selected by the employer. You would anticipate that there should be some time limit set that would include not only a treatment plan but a return-to-work plan.

Perhaps an employee should first be required to utilize all personal and banked holiday time. If they still requested additional time off, perhaps the CO or chief of police could grant them a set, additional period of recovery or treatment time. If the employee still felt unable to return to work, I believe that any additional time off should, if granted at all, be in the form of leave without pay.

Obviously, significantly more latitude should be given to an officer who has been involved in a work, life or health event that is identifiable and would be expected to result in anyone suffering from stress. But even so, it's hard to imagine an event that would require months or years of stress leave. Employees have lost spouses, children and parents or gone through family break ups and returned to work in days or weeks. Employees have suffered with cancer, surgery or other significant medical issues and returned to work within weeks or months. Many officers involved in shootings, traumatic incidents, violent assaults or other work related incidents either miss no work or very little.

If it's hard for most officers to understand what type of incident might require stress leave spanning months and years, imagine how the public must view it.

A STORY OF REAL STRESS: WITHOUT PAY OR BENEFITS

I have a very good friend who has her own mortgage business. She's a tiny slip of a thing barely weighing 100 lbs. Several years ago she had her first child. About two weeks later she was back at work. When I asked her why she was back so quickly, she replied, "Because I don't get paid to be at home." A year or so later she had a second child and about two weeks later she again returned to work. Same thing, I asked her why so quick and her answer was the same, "Because I don't get paid to be at home."

Within a very short time, my friend discovered that both of her children were special needs and that one of them had severe autism. In spite of this devastating news, she just kept moving ahead. It was incredible. Her husband was a logger and was away from home for days and weeks at a time. She worked full time and cared for two special needs children, often on her own. And she just kept moving forward.

In the spring of 2012, my friend received the traumatic news that her husband had been killed in a logging accident. She was devastated. Everyone who knew her and her story was devastated. We attended the funeral and watched as she gathered her children and faced the ordeal with a courage that simply inspired awe. And she just kept moving forward.

Two weeks later I walked into the office and there she was, back at work. This time I didn't ask her why. I knew the answer.

If ever there was a person who deserved stress leave, it was my friend. If ever a person had a reason to break down and give up, it was my friend. But she never gave up. She just kept moving forward.

I hope that any person who is abusing the system, taking stress leave because of some perceived slight, because they are unhappy with work, a colleague, supervisor or the department, reads this and are ashamed of themselves. If they have discovered that police work is not the occupation for them then fine, there's no shame in that. Resign and move on to some other occupation. Don't cheat the system, collect your paycheque and leave your colleagues to bear the weight that you should be sharing. Don't be a paper officer who exists only in some administrative file.

14

HIRING OF POLICE OFFICERS

The goal should be to hire the best that society offers,
for who they hire and how they hire will have a critical,
long-term effect on all police departments and will
ultimately contribute to their successes and
their failures.

While it may seem, at first glance, that a chapter on the hiring of
police officers would be of little or no interest to the non-police
reader, I'd like to offer a different perspective. Who is hired,
and how police officers are hired has a significant impact on the
quality of police service that a community will receive and this
should be of interest to everyone.

So just who are police recruits, and how do we hire police
officers? Police recruits are a cross section of society and the age
group or generation from which they are selected, and they will
bring with them the values, attitudes and work ethics common
to their peers. As history and experience has shown, those traits
may vary from one age group to another, from one culture to
another or even from one gender to another.

This creates a challenge for recruits and for departments
when it comes to personnel management and training. If a supervisor is operating from a different set of values, attitudes and
work ethic than the recruit it can result in conflict. It then must
be asked, should the supervisor adapt to the new recruit or must

the new recruit adapt to the supervisor? You may not be surprised to find the answer is that both need to adapt.

New recruits can learn many valuable things from supervisors and other experienced officers, but they also bring something of their own to the table. Fresh attitudes, new techniques, better education and different perspectives can be a huge asset to any police department. Recruits should be encouraged to discuss new ideas, challenge old ways of doing things and to offer differing opinions and suggestions. Certainly, at the end of the day, it must be the supervisor who makes the final decision, but it would be counter-productive to ignore everything that a recruit has to offer.

Another thing to consider about the goal of getting the best society has to offer is, who are the candidates that comprise the pool from which police departments hire? Clearly, the larger the pool of candidates, the better the quality of recruits, and there are several factors that determine this.

One is that this pool will only contain those people who actually want to be police officers. This may seem so obvious as to not bear mentioning but what is not so simple are the factors that may affect this. Are the pay and benefits sufficient given the responsibilities, liabilities, conditions and hours of work and the consequences of making a mistake? How are police officers and police departments perceived by the public they serve and will this perception have a positive or negative influence on potential candidates? This of course can be influenced by the media and by the public relations policy of the police department and will be discussed later in more detail.

A second factor that determines the pool of candidates is the police department's policy in regards to selective or affirmative hiring based on things like gender, language, race, culture and education. Clearly there is huge benefit to any police department to have qualified recruits from all strata of the communities which they police. *Having an educated, multi cultural, gender balanced roster should be the goal of every police department.* The question then becomes, how should this be done?

I believe that police departments should, at all costs avoid *targeted hiring* and focus on *targeted recruiting.* . .and there is a big difference.

Targeted *hiring* implies that only recruits (or a disproportionate number at least), will be hired from select gender, racial or cultural pools and to my mind that is not only counter-productive but harmful in the long term. It can cause resentment amongst current personnel. It puts additional pressure on the new recruit by calling into question their qualifications, however fine they may be. It may cause other qualified candidates to move onto other careers and, in some cases, actually result in a lesser or perhaps even unqualified candidate being hired.

Targeted *recruiting*, on the other hand, can be a valuable process. If police departments aggressively advertise and recruit so as to attract qualified candidates of all genders, races and cultures and make it known that everyone is welcomed and encouraged to apply it can only benefit the entire department. No department will be criticized for attempting to recruit on universities and campuses. No department should be criticized for recruitment which is targeted at the various racial and cultural groups within the community they police. The value of having officers versed in the languages and cultures of the general public cannot be overstated.

In the past, much of the screening process for potential candidates involved de-selection or the screening out of candidates who did not have the required characteristics, traits or background. Many departments are now starting to include a more proactive process. They still eliminate candidates with undesirable qualities, but also focus heavily on candidates who have those qualities which have proven to be present in successful and valued police officers. In other words, they choose candidates who fit the emotional and psychological profile that has been determined to be common in *good* officers.

This would seem to make an abundant amount of sense and should form a basis for hiring all future candidates. Certainly, the most important criteria is that all candidates *must* have high standards of honesty and integrity, they *must* be fully qualified and they must be *perceived* as being qualified by both the public and by other officers.

15

PROMOTING POLICE OFFICERS

The North American ideal, if unchecked, will lead to the logical conclusion of not only prohibiting discrimination on the grounds of race, religion and color, but also on ability.

It's difficult to write this type of book without straying into some areas and topics that may seem more directed to police officers than to non-police officers. There is no question that this may be one of those topics; however, I would ask you to consider the very real impact that police supervisors have on the overall level and quality of police service in any community. It is vital that the right officers are promoted into the right job functions and for this reason alone you may discover some of the topics discussed in this chapter to be of interest. If nothing else, I hope it provokes discussion and thought.

For many employees, one of the benefits of working within a larger organization is the opportunity for promotion or advancement. Rightly or wrongly, in North America, success is often associated with job status and so it is with most police departments. As in any endeavor, competition for promotional positions can be intense and often results in two things. One is that a disproportionate amount of employee time and energy can be focused on preparing for promotional requirements. Secondly, is that a disproportionate amount of employee and employer time and energy can be focused on dealing with the grievances, disappointments and resentment of the unsuccessful candidates.

Almost every organization will have some form of rank or managerial structure which allows for various levels of supervision and responsibility. The quality of the employees who fill these supervisory positions is of critical importance to the efficiency and success of the entire organization. For this reason, the goal of most police departments should certainly be to promote the best candidate possible, and much time and effort has been put into trying to achieve this.

There are systems to identify candidates, to select candidates, to eliminate candidates and to hear appeals and grievances. There are systems within systems. Departments have used exams, interviews, performance evaluations, peer reviews and combinations of all. Many organizations have tried a variety of systems, changing every few years in search of the elusive "perfect system." It's a search doomed to failure. . .because it doesn't exist.

The reason it doesn't exist is that there are far too many subjective variables and very few reliable, objective and measurable ones. For example, relying solely on an exam score ignores the importance of interpersonal skills. Many top employers now recognize the value of EQ, or emotional quotient as being more important than IQ. In fact, studies have shown that over 90% of high performers have high levels of EQ. Conversely, relying solely on interpersonal skills may ignore a candidate's lack of job knowledge or experience.

Interviews are highly subjective and overly dependent on the employee's performance in that one interview. Seniority alone offers no incentive to either senior or junior employees who may take the position that promotion is simply a matter of time. It also ignores individual capabilities, both positive and negative in that a senior employee may be a poor performer and a more junior employee a very high performer.

While the use of performance evaluations may seem like a reliable and efficient method, it is in fact fundamentally flawed. The true value of a performance evaluation, when properly completed, is to provide an employee with valuable and constructive feedback relating to his job function. Almost every employee will have some strengths and some weaknesses and could benefit considerably if this was indicated to them. However, when used for the purposes of determining promotional qualities, the evaluation simply becomes a competitive tool. Knowing this, some supervisors will, either out of loyalty or to avoid disputes, score their subordinates with artificially high evaluations. This means that subordinates of supervisors who do not do this are at a competitive disadvantage and may have legitimate grievances.

Thus the employee evaluation, meant as a developmental tool but used as a promotional tool, will have been rendered useless and unreliable for either purpose.

So then, what can an organization do if they wish to promote the best candidates? To answer this we have to discuss the two primary theories pertaining to human performance, the Bell Curve and the Power Law.

BELL CURVE

For many years it has been widely held that human performance would follow a Bell Curve and that a group of employees could be categorized as approximately 15–20% being very high performers, 15–20% very poor performers and 60–70% ranging from low average to high average. This is still the normal standard used for this purpose.

POWER LAW

In 2012, researchers Ernest Boyle and Herman Aquinis conducted five studies involving 633,263 people in the entertainment, sports, scientific and political fields. What they discovered was that 94% of those studied followed the Power Law distribution more closely than the Bell Curve distribution. The Power Law is an extremely complex scientific equation and I have no intention or ability to, describe it.

However, what Boyle and Aquinas determined is that in any large group within a particular field or occupation, there will consistently be a sizable number of elite performers with the majority performing below the mathematical average. They used an example that approximately 66% of Major League baseball players commit more errors than average. The same results were found to apply when 490,185 scientists/researchers were the subjects. It was noted however, that determining averages carries some risk and used as an example workplace wages where an average wage might be significantly affected by very high wages at one end of the spectrum or very low wages at the other.

As mentioned earlier, in the past, police departments have used all sorts and types of criteria in an attempt to promote the best candidate with the problem being the lack of valid, quantifiable, measurable or absolute factors that might be used. If one looks at both studies, it is noted that each points out the presence of at least two significant groups or categories of employee. The Power Law indicates there are two: *the elite and the rest*. The Bell Curve suggests there are three: *the significantly above average, the average and the significantly below average*. This information may act as a guide for departments searching for a way to narrow the field or pool of candidates from which they will choose.

Both studies would suggest that the real goal of a promotion process should be to identify the top performers, the average performers and the low performers. It follows that the second goal would then be to determine how to best select the most qualified candidate. In other words, to establish three very important objectives and criteria:

1. To develop standards that would allow for both the elite and the very poor performers within the department to be identified.

2. To determine minimum standards that *every* employee must meet to be considered for promotion. This might include years of service, the passing of an exam or any other criteria that a particular department may deem as a minimum standard.

3. To determine minimum standards required for a supervisory position in the various job functions within a department. Again, this might be years of service, the passing of an additional exam or a certain amount of experience in that particular job or duty function.

If this was accomplished, departments could then create three categories of employee, those being highly promotable, generally promotable, and not promotable.

Highly Promotable

This list would be comprised of those employees who had been identified as elite or high performers and who had achieved the minimum standards for promotion as identified by the department.

Generally Promotable

This would include the balance of employees who had achieved the required minimum standards.

Not Promotable

This list would include employees who had been identified as very poor performers, those who have not yet attained the required minimum standards or those who have indicated that they do not wish to be promoted.

Application

Individual employees within the two promotable groups should be listed by seniority. While this may seem contrary to what has been discussed, it really isn't. Once the candidates have been selected for each list, it is virtually impossible to further separate or rank individuals using any other objective criteria and attempting to do so would create significant turmoil. Seniority then becomes the most measurable, least subjective criteria left. If the process of creating the lists has been properly applied, the successful candidate will be of high caliber regardless. At the very least, seniority would be a difficult criteria to challenge simply because it is measurable and finite.

When a promotional position became available, the department should simply go to the Highly Promotable list and, by seniority, select the first candidate who fits all of the minimum requirements for that particular job. Should that employee turn it down for any reason, simply move to the next and so on until an employee accepts the job position. Should no employee on the Highly Promotable list accept or be qualified for the position, then the department would move onto the Generally Promotable list and start the process again. Departments having a need to staff various geographic locations might consider allowing only a limited number of refusals of promotional positions before removing the candidate to the generally promotable list, thus ensuring employee mobility.

It should be understood that employees may move from one category to another. For example, officers who did not meet the minimum standards required for promotion may have now achieved the level of service or exam mark that would make them promotable. A lower achiever may improve or a high achiever may do something that would require they be removed from the highly promotable list. Also, an employee who had once indicated no interest in the promotion process may wish to change that status. It must also be considered that not every employee will successfully transform from worker to a manager and that recently promoted individuals should be monitored to ensure they remain deserving of a highly promotable rating.

All of this raises the inevitable question. How should departments select candidates for each list and remain fair and transparent? While this is certainly not my area of expertise, there are a few thoughts that may be worth exploring.

Experts agree that past performance is a good indicator of future performance. This is especially true if performance is measured over time and a variety of conditions. Conditions in this case might include different job functions, different supervisors or various colleagues. If an employee was consistently rated as exceptional by different supervisors and colleagues, all while performing different job functions, this would be a very strong indicator of future performance.

There are any number of human resource experts who can identify the characteristics of highly successful employees and supervisors. Generally they include such things as highly motivated, loyal, reliable, responsible, requiring little supervision and respected by supervisors and peers. They also include the ability and willingness to self evaluate, take responsibility for errors, share credit with peers and to exhibit leadership and team building skills.

Supervisors at any level should be allowed to identify a potentially elite employee and recommend them to the next level of management or to the HR department. The recommending supervisor should be required to provide substantial evidence to support this evaluation including input and opinions from other supervisors and colleagues. The recommendation should be fully supported by at least one other supervisor in the employee's chain of command.

If the employee is currently not promotable for other reasons, the recommendation should be placed on file and reviewed annually. If an employee has achieved the minimum standards for promotion and receives such an endorsement, the HR department should thoroughly review the employee's file. Considerable weight should be given to multiple recommendations, especially from different supervisors and colleagues. It would also be very relevant if an employee had been consistently recommended for a number of years. Based on this information, the employee would be approved or not approved for placement on a particular list.

Should an employee be rated as not promotable due to job performance, behavior, attitude or other factors, a supervisor should be required to provide significant evidence in support of the reasons for this rating. This might include such things as disciplinary records, *specific* examples of attitude or performance issues, substance abuse or personal issues or interpersonal problems with supervisors or colleagues. Again, this assessment should be supported by at least one other supervisor in the employee's chain of command.

It would be important to review employee status annually as an employee may significantly improve their position in a variety of ways including additional education, a successful response to discipline or treatment, a life or attitude change or many other factors. The same might also apply to an employee in reverse.

It must be recognized that the transition from employee to supervisor often involves significantly different skills, knowledge and responsibilities than may have been required in the previous job role. It should not be assumed that the promoted candidate will automatically acquire those skill sets or knowledge without some training or instruction specific to these new responsibilities. *I don't think this can be overstated.*

Every police department would be very well served by developing effective promotional training courses available either via classroom setting, DVD or online and every officer that is promoted should be required to successfully complete it prior to assuming their new role. This course should thoroughly discuss the responsibilities and expectations related to their new supervisory position. This would include a full understanding of the department's standards, policies and procedures for dealing with such things as workplace conflict, disciplinary matters, mentoring and coaching, complaint resolution and a host of other topics pertaining to their role. This might well provide for a more consistent application of those various standards, policies and procedures from one supervisor to the next. If the new responsibilities include supervision of municipal or other union-ized employees, they must be made aware of the provisions of any collective bargaining agreements that would be relevant.

It would seem that if a department is prepared to go to great lengths to ensure the proper candidate is selected, then it would follow that they should take the additional step of ensuring they had the required tools, skills and knowledge to become successful supervisors. If chosen properly, the candidate will already possess the work ethic, attitude and interpersonal skills necessary to become a good supervisor. The value in providing that candidate with the additional training is that they will likely become *excellent* supervisors!

As has already been pointed out, there is no perfect system. There is no doubt that creating lists, tiers or rankings of employees will create some hard feelings, resentment and disappointment. It may mean that some employees will never be promoted. But if employees understood the system and what characteristics and criteria were used in the selection process, it might also result in employees making significant efforts to improve their positions. Regardless, a professional organization such as a police department is not some game or activity where everyone gets their turn or wins a prize. The stakes are simply too high.

Who departments promote will have an incredible and long lasting influence on how subordinates develop and on the future success of the entire department. One or two bad employees can be absorbed and dealt with. *One or two bad supervisors however, can create extensive damage and legacy of problems and harm to a department.*

16

PAYING THE HUMAN TOLL

They say time heals all wounds. I wonder who "they" are?

———

The devil cried, "All pay the toll, for no one rides for free"
When a man with a badge stepped forth and said, "Give the bill to me"
And Satan howled and pawed the ground and swore that man would pay
So he cursed all men who wore a badge and the curse still holds today

So when you see those haunted eyes and the lines upon his face
Know Satan wants his debt repaid, his price the human race
But he can't collect, he can't foreclose, the debt is kept at bay
Cause a man with a badge makes the payment and he makes it every day

Yes Satan's bill's still on the books, still being paid for now
By a man with a badge and jaded eyes and lines upon his brow
But you'll ride safe on the road of life, safe by a promise made
By a man who paid the devil's price and said "Your toll is paid"

by Wayne Ryan

———

A lot has been written and documented about the long-term effects of combat experience in the military and it is generally agreed that most soldiers who have seen active combat will experience some form of Post-Traumatic Stress Disorder (PTSD). In some cases it may be mild and have no measurable effect on their lives and in some cases it is severe to the point of debilitating.

When one considers the inhumanity they witness, the violent, brutal deaths that occur around them, the acute stress caused by very real danger of personal death or injury and the stress caused when a human being is forced to kill or potentially kill another human being, it would be surprising if there was not some form of mental and emotional trauma.

The US military reports that approximately 30% of military personnel will experience significant PTSD. Can it be strictly coincidental then, that in a war situation, only approximately one third or 33% of US military personnel are in actual combat positions, with the rest in non-combat, support positions?

Much less has been studied or reported about the long-term effects of stress as applied to those in law enforcement. This is strange given the statistics which reveal that police officers have such high rates of divorce, alcohol abuse, depression and suicide.

Why would some of societies best young men and women fall victim to these pitfalls? The answer may well be found in some of the research that *has* been done...

STRESS OF POLICE WORK

"Law enforcement is the most stressful occupation in North America, even surpassing the formidable stress of air traffic controllers."
— **Hans Selye, world's foremost workplace stress researcher**

"Law enforcement is the most psychologically dangerous job in the world."
— **Dr. Hans Toch, author, *Stress in Policing***

"Rates of alcohol abuse are approximately double in the policing community as that of the general public."
— **J.M. Violanti, FBI Law Enforcement Bulletin**

Larry Beutler and associates P. Nussbaum and K. Meredith published a study, *Changing Personality Patterns of Police Officers,* in which 25 police officers were evaluated at or shortly after their recruitment and again two years later. Eleven of the officers were available for follow-up four years after recruitment. Minnesota Multiphasic Personality Inventory (MMPI) scores showed significant changes over time, suggesting increasing somatic symptoms, anxiety, and alcohol vulnerability. The increased vulnerability to alcohol abuse was the strongest finding, and by the fourth year of service, mean MacAndrews Alcoholism Scale scores were within the critical range. (Professional Psychology: Research and Practice, Volume 19(5), Oct 1988, 503-507)

Examples of Trauma-causing Incidents

Noted psychologist Dr. Nancy Davis has identified the following incidents as most apt to be potentially traumatic for law enforcement officers. In no particular order:

- A reasonable belief that the officer's death or critical injury was imminent.

- Accidentally killing or wounding a bystander.
- The officer's inability to stop a suspect from injuring or killing another.
- Killing or wounding a child, teenager or mentally ill individual, even if the life of the officer had been threatened.
- Viewing the body of a child victim, particularly if the officer has children, or if the child had been assaulted, abused or tortured.
- When a dead victim becomes personalized, rather than just an unknown body.
- The terror of being caught in a violent riot.
- An officer is blamed or told he or she is responsible for the death of an innocent bystander, law enforcement officer, or a child victim.
- Particularly bloody or gruesome scenes that involve decay, dismemberment, or suffering.
- Observing an event involving violence or murder or suicide.
- Feeling responsible for someone else's life (hostage negotiators).
- Being involved in dangerous situations such as high risk chases, arrests or searches.
- Undercover assignments in which the officer is constantly "on-guard" because of the likelihood of being hurt, killed, or discovered.
- Viable threats of violence by suspects towards an officer and/or his or her family.
- Witnessing the death of a law enforcement officer or viewing their body at the scene.

While this list may not be comprehensive, and there are certainly some situations listed which very few officers would rarely, if ever, have to deal with, there are also many that are a routine part of any operational police officer's normal duties. As with the military, not all police officers work in the type of operational duties that would expose them to many of the trauma causing events on this list. But those officers in uniform patrol duties, homicide, robbery, traffic duties, emergency response units, hostage negotiation, gang units, street enforcement units, organized crime and other operational units will all very likely experience any number of those events, often many times over their careers.

In fact, I would say that when you consider that most combat soldiers may serve one to three years and only spend a relatively small amount of that time in actual combat, there are many police officers who, depending upon duty assignments, will see and experience more death, pain, suffering and inhumanity than most military personnel, including combat soldiers, would ever see or experience.

The information from these noted sources is sobering. Putting it into perspective, it's not hard to imagine that many officers will experience some degree of PTSD in their lives, and as mentioned earlier, it can have a wide range of effects. What has also been recently discovered, primarily with Vietnam veterans, is that sometimes the symptoms don't appear until many years after the event or events that caused them.

I do believe that in many cases, police officers instinctively learn how to cope with many of the traumatic events they experience. Unlike the combat soldier, who is literally thrown into and out of intense, immediate, kill-or-be-killed situations that may last for a relatively short time before starting again, a police officer generally experiences trauma over a much longer period of time. This may provide an opportunity for some to almost *adapt* to it and thus minimize the effects. There can however be a cost for this as well.

Officers may learn how to internalize and control their emotions at the risk of becoming too emotionless. They may learn to use cynicism to guard against disappointment and risk an inability to trust. They might become desensitized at the risk of becoming insensitive. And they may learn to hide their fear or pain at the risk of hiding other feelings.

Some of these effects become so ingrained over the years that they never really disappear. Like the mother who sends her boy to war and is shocked at the man who returns, so it may be with police officers. Can anyone remain the same, untouched and unaffected by a career filled with so much death, pain, suffering and evil? I have been retired from policing for several years and I will share my story.

My entire career was spent in operational policing. During that time I witnessed much death and human suffering. I have witnessed literally every *form* of death one could imagine, from natural causes and suicides, to accidents and homicides. I have also witnessed almost every *manner* of death from non-violent to total body dismemberment. I have witnessed the torture and death of children, sexual abuse, rape, murder for hire, premeditated murder, mass murder, entire families murdered, husbands killing wives and vise versa. I have experienced situations where I faced imminent serious injury or death and situations where I faced the possibility of causing serious injury or death to another. The list is simply too long to go on.

For the most part I feel that I have dealt with it very well. I have a loving family, good friends and a good life. I don't abuse alcohol or drugs, am not depressed or angry and in general feel quite well adjusted. But I have not forgotten. . .

THE PSYCHOPATH AND THE BIRTHDAY PARTY

While working on the Serious Crime Unit at Surrey Detachment in 1994 we received a call about a homicide at a residence. As we arrived at the house, I noted that it was a quiet, residential neighborhood with tree lined streets and well-kept homes and yards. As we entered, I immediately noticed several things. The house was beautifully decorated with ribbons and balloons indicating a birthday party for a six-year-old girl. The house was very neat, tidy and well kept. There was an upright vacuum cleaner standing in the kitchen. And there was a dead woman lying on the kitchen floor with multiple stab wounds.

As we began to look around, I observed a small amount of blood on the stairs leading to the upper portion of the home. As we climbed the stairs, the blood pattern became slightly larger, and as we got to the top of the stairs it clearly led to a closed bedroom door. I remember approaching that door, knowing what I would see, preparing for the worst, and still hoping for a miracle. And I remember opening that door to a sight that haunts me still.

A little six-year-old girl in her party dress. Lying on her back, her eyes staring sightlessly at the ceiling. And my heart broke. I remember the lump in my throat and fighting the tears. Stupidly, I recall thinking that for God's sake, I was a homicide investigator, to buck up and do my job. I remember having to go outside to regain my composure. And I have never forgotten.

Subsequent investigation revealed that the victim and her daughter lived in the house and that she had decorated it in preparation for her daughter's sixth birthday party. Reconstruction of the scene showed that the mother had been in the kitchen vacuuming when she'd been attacked. It appeared that the little girl had attempted to escape up the stairs and received the first knife wound as she ran. The killer then followed her into her room and stabbed her so hard in the chest that the shape of the knife's hilt was deeply imprinted in her breastbone.

We were able to determine that the mother had recently befriended a man who had spent some time in prison. Friends and neighbors described her as the sort of person who would always take in a stray animal or befriend a stray person. As this male had been seen at the house earlier and the victim's car was missing, we put out a search and locate request for him and the car.

A short while later we received information from one of this male's associates indicating that he had stolen a car in Surrey with the intention of doing a drug rip off in a nearby community, and that he was planning to kill the victims during this rip off. Police in the neighboring area were notified and quickly located the suspect and vehicle. When they attempted to pull him over he fled and during the chase, fired several shots at police. He was ultimately arrested without injury and I was called to pick him up and transport him back to Surrey.

One of my strengths or skill sets as a police officer was an ability to interview suspects and develop enough of a rapport that they would often talk or offer confessions. By this time I had interviewed hundreds of people, many of them for major crimes like homicide, and felt that I had complete control over my emotions in those types of situations.

As I and another officer prepared to enter the interview room we checked our firearms into a locker, as was policy. We entered the room and the suspect was already seated. I remember that his eyes were totally flat and lifeless, and reminded me of a shark's as it circles the tank. Just watching and waiting for its chance.

I began talking to the suspect, trying to develop some connection or illicit some basic human reaction. And he simply sat there, staring. I tried using facts and logic and he sat there. Then I tried using emotion and guilt about this woman who had befriended him, and the little girl who had never harmed a soul. At this, the suspect made his first and only response. He yawned and asked, "When do they serve food here?"

I literally felt the blood drain out of my face. My partner later told me I had gone instantly white. Then I felt a rage like I have never felt before or since. I started to physically tremble and time seemed to freeze. And I thanked God I had left my gun outside in that locker...because I had never wanted to hurt or kill anyone, ever, the way I wanted to kill him.

I'm still uncertain just how I managed to get up and leave that room without attacking him. And I remember to this day, feeling that I had failed, that I had let him win because I hadn't been able to control my emotions. I also learned an uncomfortable thing about myself that day: That I could have executed another human being without regret or the loss of a single night's sleep.

The suspect was eventually sentenced to life in prison where, sadly, he stabbed and seriously injured a prison guard several years later.

How has this affected me? I can tell you that I have never forgotten that little six-year-old girl lying there in her room. I can tell you that I have never forgotten the feeling of rage and frustration I felt when interviewing that suspect or the deep-down knowledge that I could have executed another human being. I have never, not even one time, walked into a house or room that is decorated with ribbons and balloons without remembering that day.

THE SMELL OF VAPORUB

When investigating homicides, it was not uncommon to attend a crime scene or autopsy where a body had been undiscovered for several days and had begun to decay. As one might imagine, the odor could get extreme so we all carried Vicks VapoRub and would dab it under our noses in those circumstances. Flash forward several years and I am long retired. One day I bent down to pick up my three-year-old granddaughter. She had been suffering with a cold and unbeknownst to me her mother had spread Vicks VapoRub on her chest. When I picked her up and smelled the Vicks it was like a floodgate opened and all these long forgotten memories re-surfaced.

It was amazing how a simple smell could have that effect so many years later. It didn't last long and had no serious consequences but it does make you wonder how deeply set some of those experiences and memories really are.

A GRUESOME FIND

Surrey Detachment received a report of a woman who had gone missing under very suspicious circumstances. When last seen by her friend the previous day, she had been going to a house party at a Surrey location and she had not been seen or heard from since. She was working as a prostitute and had a serious drug addiction, but in spite of her life style, she was apparently reliable in this regard and her friends and family were very concerned.

Given the circumstances, the file was turned over to the Serious Crimes Section and an investigation commenced. When we attended the house where she had allegedly gone to party, we discovered two males, neither of them being Citizen of the Year candidates. The house was a total mess with clothing, rotting food and debris all over. Neither male was very co-operative but did say the missing woman had been there for a short while and left alone. They said they had not seen her since.

They gave us permission to look around and we did so. I discovered a motorcycle helmet lying amidst a pile of junk and noted minute flecks of red on the face mask but had no way of identifying what it was. As we had no grounds to search or seize and certainly no basis on which to arrest either of the males, we departed and continued our investigation.

While proceeding with all the normal avenues, we began questioning known associates of these two males and that's when we got our first break. One of these associates reacted strangely to my questions, becoming fidgety and nervous. By this point in my career I had interviewed literally hundreds of suspects in a variety of crimes and quickly sensed that something was going on with this subject. It didn't take long before he told me what it was. A part of me has wished ever since that he had not.

For anyone who has never seen a grown man sob uncontrollably, it can be disconcerting. To watch a hardened criminal do it is downright alarming. When he calmed down enough to continue, the story he told was simply bone chilling.

He advised that he had received a call the day before from one of the males we'd spoken to at the house earlier and was asked to come over to help with something. When he got there he discovered the body of a female lying on the bedroom floor and it was obvious that she had been dead for some time. The males told him that she had died of a drug overdose and they needed his help in getting rid of the body. When he asked them why they didn't just call an ambulance, they indicated that they didn't want any police involvement because of the drug angle.

He agreed to help and they waited until dark before loading her into the trunk of his car. He advised us that they had a very difficult time getting her body into the trunk because rigor mortis had made all of her limbs stiff and almost impossible to bend. Apparently the other male told the subject to wait in the car while he got a shovel and some things they would need. Once he was done, they drove to a deserted area and prepared to unload her. Upon opening the trunk he observed the body as well as a shovel, motorcycle helmet and a chainsaw.

The subject was shocked and began to object, but was in fact frightened of this male and decided to do what he was told, which was to begin digging a grave. As he did so, the other male put the motorcycle helmet on, lowered the face shield and began to dissect the body into pieces. He decapitated her, cut each arm into two pieces and each leg into three. He then produced some garbage bags and asked the subject to assist in putting the body parts into them. At this point the subject was physically ill and unable to assist. The other male finished up and together they buried the bags in the grave that had been dug and returned to the house. They washed the blood off of the helmet and chainsaw, the male disposed of all clothing in a dumpster somewhere and the subject departed after being warned to keep his mouth shut.

Based on his statement, we were able to arrest the suspects, execute a search warrant on the premises and seize the motorcycle helmet and chainsaw. Lab tests would later verify that the victim's blood was on both.

It fell to me to accompany the subject to the grave site and recover the remains. That is an experience I would not wish on anyone — ever! I can still recall working with the pathologist and assisting him in rearranging the victim on the operating table. Thinking that of all the indignities suffered by this poor lost soul in her life, this final one must have been the worst.

As a side note: The autopsy determined that the victim had been strangled. Based on that information, we were able to obtain a confession from one of the suspects and both were convicted of second degree murder and sentenced to lengthy prison time.

I didn't have a break down, get drunk or sink into a depression. I didn't really react at all, and that in itself tells a story. I was just numb. Numb with what I had seen. Numb with realizing the depths of human depravity. And numb with the knowledge that what I had experienced that day had become a part of me. . .and that there was nothing I could do about it.

———

As I indicated earlier, I don't in any way consider myself damaged or debilitated from my experience as a police officer, but there are residual effects. Because of the major issues that I have seen and dealt with, I'm told that I have a tendency to treat many of life's normal issues as minor and unimportant. That of course, is potentially hurtful to friends and loved ones, as it can minimize what they are feeling or experiencing and it's something I continually work on.

In any sort of argument or confrontation, my wife tells me I go into *"cop mode"* where I emotionally disengage, become dispassionate and attempt to control the situation. There are times when memory cues such as the Vicks, something on TV or driving past an old homicide scene will cause a "flashback" and I will vividly recall physical and emotional details. Are these mild symptoms of PTSD or just normal, human memory responses and reactions? Perhaps a bit of both.

———

I suspect that many of the things I have mentioned here are experienced by most operational police officers to one degree or another. There is little doubt that different people will be affected differently, some minimally and some seriously. I do however believe, that it would be almost impossible to spend a career in law enforcement and leave completely unchanged.

Of course, it absolutely must be said, that while many of the stories and scenarios in this book have been tragic or dramatic, the purpose was to make or support a point or opinion. There are also many events and incidents in law enforcement that are humorous and heart warming. For every criminal that makes you lose faith in humanity, you meet five great people who restore it. Those are the 80% that make it all worth it.

Yes, law enforcement changes a person. But much of that change is positive. Certainly many of the values, lessons, attitudes and opinions formed and learned as a police officer stay with most of us for the rest of our lives. Call me biased, but I believe, generally speaking, that's a good thing!

17

THE MEDIA AND THE POLICE

The police and the media have an uneasy alliance
for they are both friend and foe!

Having a free press is integral to having a free society and its importance can't be overstated. Having said that, an independent, impartial police force that has the support and the trust of the public is just as important and I wonder sometimes if this gets lost in all the clutter. It's in this balance that we discover the truth. . .that the police and the media form an uneasy alliance as both friend and foe.

When considering the relationship between police and the media it is very important, in my opinion, to keep one thing in mind at all times. *The media is not the public.* They do not speak for the public and they do not represent the public. The media is, to a large extent, an entertainment business. They make their money based on how well they entertain the public and it would be naïve to believe that they are simply focused on providing the public with all of the facts or the entire story.

If the modern day media is much more about entertainment than actual news reporting, how can this cause problems from a policing perspective? Unfortunately, when it comes to the media, the reporting of inappropriate behavior, mistakes, internal disputes or complaints involving police organizations is so tempting because it is entertaining. After all, who doesn't like watching the referee take a fall?

The entertainment value of a police-involved incident is high and will always receive a great deal of media attention. This, combined with the need to break the story first, often results in news reports which are inaccurate, out of context or which fail to tell the entire story. By the time the entire story is known, the entertainment factor is gone and the media have moved on to the next story. This can leave the public with the wrong perception of what occurred or without the full details necessary to put the incident into the proper context.

When it comes to policing, does the media have a responsibility to report all the facts in a balanced manner? To report the good with the bad? What public need gets met if the media portrays policing in such a consistently negative manner that potentially good candidates decide on a different career path, when experienced officers leave for other employment, when public confidence is eroded and when disgruntled employees find a sympathetic and very public method of airing their grievances?

It's not hard to find unhappy employees in almost any large organization. Sometimes they have genuine complaints and sometimes not but the media is rarely the best way of dealing with them.

The airing or publishing of unfounded complaints or allegations by a disgruntled employee is tantamount to interviewing a person about the character of their ex-spouse. It makes for interesting gossip but nothing more.

When it comes to media coverage, should it be front-page news when a police officer is involved in an accident, a personal matter, an illicit affair or some other minor incident? Would the same coverage be given if it involved employees at another government agency or some private company?

Should a police officer be held to a higher moral and ethical standard than a priest, a politician, a judge, a doctor, a teacher, a member of the media? Why is it that if a teacher is convicted of sexually abusing a student, the incident tends to be viewed as an isolated case but if a police officer commits a crime, it reflects on the entire department? I have always been surprised at how the public and media are able to get away with making the prejudiced, generalist type of comments about our police officers and police departments that simply would not be tolerated if made about a particular race, religion or gender. In a very real sense, a uniformed police officer is the "ultimate" visible minority!

Why are many major newspapers so quick to be critical of police errors and yet almost every day are forced to print retractions and apologies for the errors made by their own reporters and editors? Do the media ever take the time to wonder why, in virtually every public opinion poll, they are ranked amongst the lowest levels, and police amongst the highest, when it comes to public trust? This, in spite of the incredible responsibility that comes with freedom of the press.

It seems to be another of our less redeeming human traits that we often hold others to a much higher standard than we hold ourselves.

Police officers are paid to enforce the law and keep the peace. They don't make the laws, they don't judge the accused and they don't sentence the guilty. They don't hold themselves out to be special or to be above normal human behavior. They're just people. Like most large organizations, there will always be a few who stumble, but most of the police officers I ever knew led exemplary professional and personal lives. Nobody likes to be tarred with the same brush when a colleague does act badly.

Yes, there are certainly times when the media is not viewed as an asset. When they interfere with investigations, insist on premature media releases, push for additional details or publish news that hinders police in doing their job. Or, when faced with deadlines, they publish what they have when they have it, leading to inaccurate, out of context reports.

Having said that, there are also many occasions where the media is a huge asset to police departments. They can broadcast police issued warnings, descriptions of vehicles, suspects and victims, promote public awareness of good news police stories and police-sponsored community programs.

Some reporters are excellent to deal with and over the years may form professional and personal friendships with officers. I know a well-respected reporter by the name of George Garrett who worked the Vancouver area for many years. He was so well liked and respected by police officers that he is still invited to many police functions in spite of the fact that he is retired. George Garrett always did his job and reported the good with the bad. If a police officer or department made a mistake, he reported it fairly and accurately and without personal bias. I think that is what garnered him the respect. He was a professional and reported all of the facts and all of the story.

CASE STUDY:
Balanced reporting?

In 2012, the media in British Columbia discovered that an Alberta RCMP officer who had been disciplined for several incidents of misconduct was being transferred to British Columbia. The story was sensational from a few perspectives. Firstly, it involved a police officer. Secondly, it involved a sexual scandal. Thirdly, it came at a time when several female RCMP officers had just gone public with allegations of sexual harassment within the force. It comes as little surprise then, that media attention was extreme and relentless. Headlines were filled with such things as "Sex Cop Exiled to BC" and "Disgraced RCMP officer to BC." The media and the public were angry and the general consensus was that this officer should have been fired. It finally got to the point that the Provincial government became involved and the commanding officer decided to hold a press conference specifically to address the issue.

So what happened? Well, simply put, an RCMP staff sergeant had admitted to seven counts of misconduct which had occurred between 2006 and 2009. This misconduct included having and consuming liquor in his office, sharing liquor with subordinates, having consensual sexual relations with two civilian subordinates, exposing himself to a co-worker and making inappropriate comments to a civilian co-worker. This officer was ultimately found guilty, fined 10 days pay and demoted one rank to sergeant. He was also transferred to British Columbia. To clarify, while a fine of 10 days pay may only be a few thousand dollars, the demotion would in effect cost this officer approximately $10,000 per year for the remainder of his career and beyond as it would affect his pension as well.

When questioned about the matter, senior officials with the Alberta RCMP stated that this officer's career record and contributions were excellent and extensive and that he had received strong letters of support from subordinates, colleagues and supervisors. His wife indicated that he had undergone a personality change after returning home from policing duties in war torn Sierra Leone. She stated that since the noted behavior, he had quit drinking, was undergoing counseling and was once again a loving husband and father.

Putting aside the more hysterical response by the media, let's examine the behavior of this officer in a more dispassionate and analytical manner in an effort to add some perspective. At this point I must clearly state that I am in no way attempting to defend or justify this officer's conduct. It is, quite frankly, indefensible. This was not just a one-time mistake, but a series of errors in judgment and behavior over a three-year period of time. The question is, was the punishment appropriate and was the media coverage fair and balanced.

Having and consuming alcohol at his office:

Certainly this is not condoned by the RCMP or most employers. I suspect, however, that if one were to search all of the desks in both private and government offices, it would not be totally surprising to find that this occurs more often than one might think. In fact, some offices have stocked bars for business or social occasions. The reports didn't specify if the drinking was done while on duty or after duty. Certainly, drinking on duty is totally unacceptable. All in all, it is clearly a bad practice and to encourage subordinates to drink at the office is poor leadership. This officer was demoted and fined 10 days pay. Is it something that would result in most senior employees being fired or would it be addressed through counseling, treatment and a lesser form of discipline with the goal being rehabilitation?

Having sexual relations with civilian subordinates:

From all accounts, the sexual contact was consensual and occurred either on lunch hour or after duty. Regarding this conduct, one has to determine what the actual offences were. Was it that this officer was married and engaged in extramarital sex? Was it that the sexual relationships were with subordinates? Was it that the incidents occurred while the officer was on duty? Speaking frankly, if the first two actions called for mandatory termination, there would be many job openings in both private and government organizations including at many of the media outlets that were so vocal in this officer's condemnation.

If it occurred while on actual duty, then it's a theft of time. If one ignores the fact that sex was involved and simply viewed it as using company time for personal activities, how much different would it be from an employee taking a day off sick when they weren't? Or leaving work early, arriving late, making personal phone calls, talking about the hockey game, taking unauthorized smoke breaks and a thousand other ways that employees steal time every day.

Having relationships with subordinates is almost always a poor idea and the negative consequences well known. It shows poor judgment and poor leadership. But should we be swayed by the fact that extra marital relationships are socially frowned upon? Is it the sexual components we find most serious or is it the theft of taxpayer funded time? Again, should it require termination of employment? Would the media generally make a practice of publishing the names and occupations of everyone involved in extramarital affairs?

Making inappropriate comments to a civilian co-worker:

From all reports, the circumstances of this were that the officer placed his arm around the co-worker and she told him she didn't like to be touched. The officer responded by asking how she and her husband had children if she didn't like to be touched. He had also referred to her as a "hottie." This was inappropriate, tasteless and crass, for sure. It's most certainly deserving of an apology and discipline. The officer was demoted and docked 10 days pay. Should this type of comment result in an employee losing their job or does it call for sensitivity training or counseling? Would the media normally report on this type of behavior?

Exposing himself to a co-worker:

There are no details about this and we are therefore unable to determine the circumstances or context of this behavior. If it was done without any mitigating circumstances, totally uninvited and criminal in nature, then that may well be the gravest of this officer's actions. If it occurred in a manner and circumstances that were mutual or invited by another party and unintentionally observed by a third party, it would still be totally inappropriate, immature and classless. This may well be the behavior most alarming to me personally.

This officer did not cover himself or the RCMP with glory when he conducted himself in this manner. His behavior certainly does not reflect the policies or procedures of the Force nor is it in any way reflective of how most officers conduct themselves. It was unprofessional, immature, inappropriate and most definitely conduct unbecoming an officer. The questions raised are several, though.

Was this officer suffering from some form of PTSD because of his experiences in Sierra Leone? Should that even matter? Did he have an alcohol abuse problem? Did his behavior and conduct meet the threshold required to support termination? Maybe the most pressing questions are: *Would the same standards of conduct apply to everyone in private and government sectors and would it have received the same level and style of media attention if it had not involved a police officer?*

CASE STUDY:
Dziekanski case and the media

For this study, we must return to the Robert Dziekanski case to illustrate the often-difficult relationship between police and the media.

When the story first broke, it was massive and dominated the news. As with any investigation, police released basic details and advised that the matter was under investigation. The media continued to demand additional information and on at least several occasions, senior officers asked to be given time to complete the investigation. Finally, at least partially in response to accusations in the media of cover ups, the RCMP made a press release providing the information that they did have. For the most part this involved what they had been told by the officers who had been involved in the incident and from witness accounts. They had still not received autopsy and laboratory results. The media continued to press and there was considerable speculation and criticism by media and the public.

Subsequent to this press release, police came into possession of a private video that had been taken of the incident. There were a few details on the video that seemed in conflict with what the officers had reported. These discrepancies largely involved the length of time that officers said they had spent with the suspect prior to using the Taser and in the video the suspect was not so much attacking the officers as waving his arms and acting agitated. When the press learned of this video's existence they went rabid, demanding that it be released immediately.

A decision was made by senior levels of the RCMP to hold off on another press release or the publishing of the tape or any other information until all of the available evidence had been collected and the investigation more complete. One can assume their reasoning was that they preferred to provide a full account of the incident rather than piecemeal or disjointed accounts that might later be found incorrect or incomplete...certainly a reasonable and logical decision.

The media did not agree. Once the investigation had been completed and the autopsy and lab results obtained, the police released the video and the fact that Mr. Dziekanski had been hit five times with the Taser. The media went ballistic. They accused the RCMP of lying to them and the public. They accused the officers of committing murder and reported that Canadians had lost faith in the RCMP. It went on and on.

What was ignored in the entire frenzy was that it had been the media themselves who had demanded early press releases. That the RCMP had asked for more time to complete their investigation and the media had accused them of cover ups and walls of silence. When senior officials released the information that their officers at the scene had reported to them, they had no reason to suspect that those accounts may have been flawed.

They simply released what they had in response to persistent demands and accusations by the media and were labeled as liars for their trouble. Given what we now know about Combat Stress Amnesia, we have to even question whether the initial reports were deliberately flawed or simply a case of memory distortion caused by acute stress. To this day, five years after the incident, the media still refers to Mr. Dziekanski's death as the day the public lost confidence in the RCMP because they had been lied to.

I have stated earlier, that if these four officers did deliberately lie to their superiors and in the public inquiry, then they deserve whatever they receive. But even if they did, these four officers do not represent the other 30,000 people that make up the RCMP. How is it fair and balanced media reporting to suggest that the entire RCMP is corrupt or lying based on the actions of four individual officers?

I don't think any police officer or department expects preferential treatment. They don't ask that bad stories never be published, mistakes never be disclosed or that police actions never be questioned. I do think they ask that they be balanced, fair, accurate and complete.

———

All of this raises an interesting question. Should police departments take a more proactive role in their own public relations?

18

PUBLIC RELATIONS

*Spinning it...the art of maximizing the good
and minimizing the bad.*

Can police departments do a better job of public relations? Certainly I think they can. For many years the generally accepted practice for police departments was to remain silent and stoic in the face of public or media criticism. In many cases, especially those involving ongoing investigations or privacy issues, they simply cannot comment. But there are other occasions when, in my opinion, a proper and timely response or rebuttal can have several positive results.

Obviously it can positively alter or effect public perception about an incident or action and that alone may be worth the effort. An added benefit, however, is that it may also have an extremely positive effect on all of the department's employees, particularly those involved in the incident. It is demoralizing and extremely stressful to officers who are unfairly or improperly portrayed in the media with no remedy available to them. If it is possible and appropriate for a department to respond on their behalf, it may well result in a stronger sense of loyalty and esprit de corps.

Conversely, there may be times where an appropriate *mea culpa* would go a long way. We already know that there will always be human error and that police officers will make mistakes, that people may be hurt or killed as a result and that sometimes there is really no sustainable defense. Perhaps that is the time to simply say to the public. . .

"We are sorry. We did not live up to your standards or our own and we are taking the necessary action to prevent it from happening again."

I believe that most of the public inherently understand that police are human and have a very difficult job to do and they are willing to forgive if they are asked to forgive! It's when they perceive that the police are attempting to avoid accountability, cover mistakes, or refuse to take responsibility for mistakes that they become angry. I suspect that the underlying reason for this anger or concern is the belief that if the police have refused to accept responsibility or to be accountable, they are, in essence, saying that they have done no wrong, and the public assumes that they will take no action to avoid or prevent the same thing from happening again and again.

Something I have often wondered about is if police departments could make better use of their retired veterans? Certainly there are times when a retired officer could say things publicly that a serving officer could not. For example, current management may not be able to comment on an ongoing investigation and therefore be unable to correct an erroneous report, explain a particular police procedure or add context to a reported incident. A retired officer may not have those same restrictions.

If a disgruntled employee were to make unfounded allegations against other officers or the department, the current management may well be unable to comment because of privacy issues, where a retired officer might not have those same constraints.

If this was to be contemplated, what would be some of the considerations? Well, in my opinion, the retired officer should be someone who held a very senior management position. The reason for that is twofold. Firstly, one of the challenges in dealing with the media is first getting their attention in such a manner that you even have an opportunity to deliver your message. They are much more likely to grant air time and newspaper space to someone who once held a high position. Secondly, a senior retired officer who has recent service would be knowledgeable, current, and able to speak with authority, thus having credibility with the public and with other officers.

Retired police chiefs, deputy chiefs, commanding officers or those holding comparable positions would be excellent candidates. They should make it plain that they are retired, not acting in any way as spokespersons or representatives of the department, and that any comments and opinions are their own. It would likely be preferable, where appropriate, if they worked in conjunction with the current senior management to avoid conflicting interests and to ensure that any factual information was accurate.

The intent of using these retired officers would certainly not be to usurp the role of the current media relations officer. The media relations officer would still be responsible for liaison with the media, release of press statements and providing investigational updates. The retired officers would act in more of a strategic role with the goal of enhancing public relations and perceptions.

If one considers that public relations is about getting positive messages out and mitigating damage caused by negative messages, it might well be to every department's advantage to at least give thought to what they could do in this regard. *If the public perception is the public reality and is determined by the information available to them, should not police departments be forging a place at the table?*

MEDIA RELATIONSHIP-BUILDING

Rick Rosenthal, a veteran TV news anchor with over 30 years of media experience and who is now a full time law enforcement consultant, offered some key strategies and tactics for winning with the media. With his permission, I am quoting liberally from an article he presented at an ILEETA conference to Force Science News and which was published in PoliceOne.com. Here are several steps he recommends for winning under such crisis conditions:

1. **Build rapport with reporters before you need it.** A major police incident is obviously a special media event, but the kind of media relationship you need to build to handle it successfully is an ongoing process that needs to begin well before a shooting occurs, Rosenthal believes. Much of the advice he offers for managing the media can be put in place and practiced beforehand, through routine, daily interactions, to build a bridge of trust and credibility. "Part of the media's job is to witness what law enforcement does, but that doesn't necessarily make them the enemy," he says. "Working with them and helping them now on other stories will give you a better chance of exercising some control over them when a crisis hits."

2. **Protect your officer and the scene.** Rosenthal opposes giving the media access to involved officers after a major incident, considering the emotional stress they're likely to be under and the potential legal ramifications of what "excited utterances" they might make. Likewise, he's firm about setting strict media limits at the scene.

"The media are not entitled to any greater right to penetrate the incident scene — don't call it a crime scene — than any other private citizen," he says. "The police get the incident scene, the media get everything beyond the taped perimeter.

"Reporters can be arrested for interfering with law enforcement if they intrude on the scene against orders, but by the same token for the police to try to control the media's movement outside the perimeter is a dreadful mistake. That opens you up immediately to charges of suppression and cover-up.

"The department spokesperson should be at the scene, all questions should be directed to him, and he should promise that the media will receive a news briefing shortly at a location of the agency's choosing, most likely away from the drama of the incident location."

3. **Provide information early and often.** In Rosenthal's opinion, talking to the media is important. "The more information they are fed after an incident," he says, "the less likely they'll go foraging on their own, finding far less knowledgeable and far less credible sources for news that is often based on innuendo, hearsay, speculation, vengeance, and biased personal opinion."

In the wake of a major incident, the media basically have a three-ply need, he says:

- Information (who, what, when, where, why, and how) and what you (your agency) are going to do about it...

- In a user-friendly form (i.e., some pithy sound bites)...

- With pictures (so the TV audience can "see what the story looks like").

He recommends that the first press briefing be held no longer than two hours after the incident. Then, depending on how "high-profile" (controversial or complex) the case is, you should follow with three formal updates per day:

- mid-morning to accommodate noon newscasts
- mid-afternoon for the evening shows
- and early evening for nighttime news filings

These briefings, conducted either by the department spokesperson or top brass, should convey as much factual information as possible, as timely as possible, without truly jeopardizing a successful investigation or possible prosecution. Despite law enforcement skepticism, he argues that most mainstream media reporters do try to be fair and accurate, and by giving them solid information, you significantly increase the probability that the truth will be printed and broadcast.

He offers these cautions to keep in mind during a briefing for reporters:

- Videotape every encounter you have with the media, whether it's a press conference or individual interview. This is good protection against being misquoted or quoted out of context.

- Avoid saying, "No comment." Verbally stonewalling or putting your hand over a camera lens makes you look guilty. "In short, you lose."

- Language that works within police circles may sound less tactful when used for a civilian audience. Calling the use of deadly force against a suspect a "good" shooting, for example, may not sit as well with some civilian sensitivities as terming it "within policy."

- The more controversial an incident is, the tougher the media questions will be. Anticipate what aggressive reporters will ask and rehearse concise, confident answers ahead of time.

4. **Be truthful and accurate.** To win with the media, give it to them straight. Any attempt to "spin" facts or speculate about the unknown will ultimately lead to accusations of cover up or pre determined results.

"If the facts of an incident are not fully known, say so. Stress that your agency always takes these matters very seriously and that a thorough investigation is underway to determine what did or did not happen. Promise that to the extent possible, you will keep the media and the public fully informed every step of the way. And in turn, ask that the media not speculate on or judge what transpired, pending confirmation of the full picture.

If you don't know the answer to a question, admit it. Promise to share that information when you do know it, if allowed to by policy, procedure, and the law.

Beware of talking 'off the record.' Don't do it, Rosenthal counsels, unless two criteria are both met: There's something important to be gained for your organization in doing so and you are fully confident in trusting the reporter involved with your professional life. Otherwise, don't take the chance."

5. **Promptly douse flaming arrows.** If it's possible to milk any controversy or air time out of a police incident, it won't be long before professional activists and aggrieved relatives of the victim try to dominate the TV cameras. "It's important to respond

immediately — in the same news cycle — to their accusations and allegations," Rosenthal says. "Every time they shoot a flaming arrow onto the tarpaper roof of your department, somebody'd better be up there putting out the fire. If you choose to say nothing, you lose."

When critics' statements can be countered with facts, clearly itemize them, he advises. When the facts are still unknown or uncertain, point out that the accusers are entitled to their opinion, but that's all it is until the investigation is complete. Encourage the media to come to you for a response before reporting outsiders' statements. Their compliance may be one of the payoffs of long-term rapport building.

If you feel you're getting the short end of biased coverage by news outlets themselves, it may help to remind media brass that reporters are expected to adhere to a detailed Code of Ethics issued by the Society of Professional Journalists. This provides specific guidelines for "seeking truth and reporting it," which specify, among other things, that distortion of the truth "is never permissible."

"Law enforcement often feels it has no recourse against mistreatment by the media, but there is accountability," Rosenthal says. "If you're treated unfairly, you need to rear up on your hind legs and fight back."

6. **Don't swat every mosquito.** In some cases, Rosenthal concedes, you may realistically be best off to ignore ethical transgressions. Bloggers, for example, aren't bound by the same restraints as professional reporters.

"They can annoy you, like a mosquito in a camping tent," he says, "but they can't really do you much harm if the facts are on your side and you argue them forcefully with the mainstream media. You need to know what bloggers are saying, but you can't swat every mosquito. If you're open, the conventional media will report what you're doing and this will be enough to significantly tip the scales in your favor."

If your incident has drawn national attention, a greater threat will be what Rosenthal calls "the down-and-out hacks from trash TV, like Nancy Grace and Geraldo Rivera." Tactics with them and their occasional local counterparts are simple. . .don't cooperate.

"What they do is spectacle, and that is not a game you should play. Odds are that cooperating with these sensationalists will be a losing proposition. You're within your rights to say no."

7. 'Fess up to UgSits. "When you mess up, 'fess up and dress up" — that's a good mantra for winning with the media when something ugly, like a bad (out of policy) shooting, occurs, Rosenthal insists. He calls such challenging events "UgSits" and says they're best met head on, not dodged. "Failing to deal with an UgSit is not an option," he says.

"Within no more than two hours from the time the first media inquiries are made, hold a full-dress news conference, confront the issue with a brief statement by your agency head, and then take questions. The longer you wait, the more time the naysayers and other critics will have to hammer you unopposed.

"You'll take hits, but don't try to defend the seemingly indefensible, justify the unjustifiable, or excuse the inexcusable. In the case of an unjustified shooting, stress that it was the behavior of an individual officer, not of the agency. Empathize with the situation and the complainants. Focus on discipline and, where appropriate, on changes in policy, procedures, and/or training."

8. **Have the patience of a saint.** "Reporters aren't stupid but they are generalists and in some cases they may be ignorant about specialty areas," such as law enforcement policies and procedures and the realities of use-of-force, Rosenthal says. Take the time and patience to educate them if they ask "dumb" questions or exhibit knowledge gaps.

"They may argue with you, repeat questions you've already answered, criticize you and the department, bait you, and frustrate you," he notes. But above all, you must not respond in kind. Ever. You must always be deliberate, calm, cool, and courteous. If you lose your head, you will become the focus of the story instead of the incident, and your outburst will inevitably end up forever on YouTube, a personal and professional nightmare."

19

POLICE TRAINING

*A mind stretched to accept new ideas today may
create new ideas tomorrow.*

As in a few other chapters, non-police readers may well find
themselves wondering why they would be interested in a topic
that appears to be strictly directed at a police audience. But I feel
strongly that proper police training is fundamental to having a
professional policing service in a community. Training standards
vary from one police department or agency to the next and in my
opinion, no discussion about policing would be complete without
including one about the training of police officers.

While police training has evolved over the years, many of
its core aspects have not. For example, most police departments
still have a process whereby a police recruit or cadet is selected
from a pool of applicants and, provided the background check
is fine, they are hired and processed through whatever training
program the department offers.

Generally speaking, this involves approximately six months
of dedicated classroom training and an additional six months or
so of working with a training officer on the job. When one considers the sheer magnitude of what a recruit must learn, it is an
incredibly short period of time. In actual fact, most experienced
officers would tell you that it takes approximately five years before
a police officer could be considered a fully seasoned, reliable and
dependable officer.

Junior officers without the requisite knowledge and experience require additional supervision and assistance. They are also prone to making the type of mistakes that result in public complaints and which require additional resources in the form of internal investigations and disciplinary action. I wonder then, if this is the most efficient model for training and if the time is coming when significant change will be required?

In considering almost all other professions, be it doctors, lawyers, teachers or accountants, you will find that an interested candidate must first go to school or university to get the necessary training and education. Only then are they eligible to be hired into that specific profession. Once hired, each profession generally has some period of onsite training such as a residency for doctors or articling for lawyers.

It does no good to earn your education degree and apply to be a doctor or to earn your law degree and apply to be an engineer. And yet that is what we tend to do with the policing profession. Candidates are often required to have at least some post secondary education, but it's rarely relevant to the actual profession of law enforcement. Even courses like criminology, psychology or sociology, while useful, are not very specific to actual police operations.

Given the critical and ever expanding role that police have in society and the sheer volume of information and knowledge that a modern police officer must have, it's actually surprising that there has been no real move to create a University-level program designed specifically for law enforcement.

Imagine a police recruit who arrived with a full knowledge of criminal law, forensics, rules of evidence, crime scene management, police tactics, investigative and arrest techniques, use of force procedures, report writing, verbal skills, public and media relations and a host of other skills and knowledge that could be imparted in a classroom. This would allow departments to concentrate their own training programs on things like self-defense, firearms training, driving skills and department specific forms, policies and procedures. Naturally, course content would be vetted for security purposes but almost all of this information is available on the internet and poses no real security risk.

I can't help but think that a candidate who has graduated from a three or four year law enforcement program might well be a fully operational, dependable and reliable officer in a much shorter time and the positive effects would likely be long term.

Certainly governments or police departments might consider sponsoring or offering scholarships to individuals, but in the end, as in most professions, should it not be the ultimate responsibility of every person interested in a career in law enforcement to obtain the required education?

Regardless of where or how training is done, there are a few topics where training and understanding might be of huge benefit to recruits and departments.

PUBLIC RELATIONS

It may sound like a strange topic for police training, but an officer who has good PR skills is a huge asset and one who does not is a huge liability. I have spoken at length about the value of public support, and this simply suggests that training in this area would enhance that support greatly.

If an officer learns the value of treating everyone, but especially those many good citizens that officers deal with every day, with professionalism and courtesy, it will have a huge positive effect.

If somehow the message could be conveyed and absorbed that officers should, in every case possible, treat those citizens the way they would want their own parents, siblings, spouses or children treated. That even when an officer is pressed for time or feels that a complaint is minor or trivial in nature, taking those few extra moments to speak or sympathize with or even allow the other party to vent would go a tremendously long way in fostering good will.

Conversely, when an officer is rude, short, dismissive or uninterested, that too will go a long way; but in the wrong direction. As everyone knows, when someone is treated well they'll tell a few people but if they're treated poorly they'll tell everyone!

If one were to summarize, it would be that one of the major training goals should be to convince all officers to be ambassadors for their departments and their profession, and to make their best effort to leave every citizen feeling better about the police after contact than before.

VIDEO AND CAMERA AWARENESS

Has anything in recent times gotten more police officers and departments into difficulty than homemade videos and photos? I don't think so. Today, almost every person over the age of eight years old has a cell phone with video and camera capability. What could possibly make a more interesting activity to video than the police arresting someone? And what will garner more media attention than a 30-second video clip of an officer or officers using unnecessary or excessive force?

Even when the excessive force used is minimal or slight, the optics are often horrible and the actions often hard or impossible to defend. *Its impact on the public is excessive because it offends their perception of how they would like their police to act.* Even when their expectations are unrealistic, perception becomes their reality. It simply must be drummed into recruits over and over again that they should anticipate and assume that anything they do or say will appear on the six o'clock news.

This same message should be repeated on a regular basis by supervisors and colleagues. It must be a *conscious consideration* in every case where police are involved in a public arrest, tactical situation, police chase or any other similar incident. It's also safest to assume that every word uttered or action taken when attending complaints, vehicle stops or other routine matters is being recorded.

CASE STUDY:
Cop-baiting in Harlem

In 2012, a 16-year-old youth in Harlem, NY decided that he would seek revenge on the police. Apparently he had been stopped and searched several times under New York's Stop and Search program. He dressed in a dark hoody and began walking up and down the street. Whenever he saw a police car, he would deliberately act in a furtive and suspicious manner, until finally a patrol car with two officers stopped him.

The youth began to deliberately bait the officers, but used no obscenity, did not resist and did nothing else that would be considered an offence. He simply used an insulting and condescending tone of voice and kept questioning the officer's right to stop and search him.

In contrast, the officers quickly lost their patience and began to speak loudly, aggressively and profanely. They eventually allowed the youth to manipulate them into physically assaulting him. And of course, the entire event was recorded.

Two experienced police officers had allowed themselves to be trapped and manipulated into an unprofessional response. To make matters worse, the youth posted the recording onto the internet where it received wide attention. With the popularity of YouTube, and with some media outlets offering substantial cash for news stories, it is almost a certainty that incidents of public videotaping will increase.

It must also be seriously considered that certain individuals will deliberately attempt to manipulate officers into compromising or perhaps even criminal actions for revenge or profit.

CONTEMPT OF COP SYNDROME

Although closely related to the previous two topics, Contempt of Cop Syndrome is significant enough to deserve its own section. Simply put, Contempt of Cop Syndrome is when a member of the public shows open disrespect, defiance or contempt or fails to show the proper level of deference to a police officer who then reacts inappropriately, either physically or verbally.

There are many different examples of this including when citizens take photos or video of officers, when they challenge their authority, call them names, taunt them or make rude motions. It might occur when onlookers accuse police of being too rough with a suspect or breaching someone's rights. In any close examination of police complaints and misconduct that are founded, it can be clearly noted that a very high percentage occur as a result of police responding inappropriately or illegally to disrespectful comments, actions or challenges to their authority.

Recruits should be cautioned about this syndrome from the earliest stages of training as it has the potential to create situations where officers make unauthorized arrests, commit assaults or engage in unprofessional interactions. They must understand that there is no general law against a citizen taking photos or video of police officers. Police officers cannot be *disturbed* in the eyes of the law. There is no law prohibiting disrespect or contempt and part of an officer's job is to deal with ignorant behavior by the public with professionalism.

So how can officers avoid falling victim to this syndrome? Well, there are a few basic rules and practices that might assist.

1. Never issue an order or command that you do not have the legal authority to enforce. Doing so leaves an officer vulnerable to being challenged and either having to back down or continue attempting to assert authority. That in turn can lead to a confrontation and the officer acting inappropriately and without legal justification.

2. If your actions are professional, no officer should fear being photographed or videotaped. It's when an officer acts or speaks inappropriately that they may feel the need to confiscate film or cameras. Since there is no law prohibiting the taking of photos or video of police officers, the officer is open to charges of misconduct or abuse of authority.

3. Never engage a citizen in a no-win conversation or argument that can escalate into a confrontation. Some in the public will make gratuitous and insulting comments with the very intention of causing an officer to react. A verbal argument with such a person has no point, no resolution and will only lead to a bad ending if allowed to occur.

4. Never use profane, insulting, dismissive or arrogant language when dealing with the public. It will almost certainly lead to a like response which can then easily get out of control. Even when it doesn't, it will demean the officer and the department. It's unprofessional and unacceptable.

5. Always remember that as a police officer you have the duty and right to keep the peace and enforce the law but you do not have the legal right to enforce respect or deference to your authority and that in virtually every Contempt of Cop incident, it will most certainly be the police officer who ultimately pays the price.

CASE STUDY: Arrest without authority

On April 8, 2006 in Denver, Colorado, a young man was walking home past a downtown parking lot when he came across two officers arresting a man. He then began videotaping the arrest. Shortly thereafter he was approached by the two officers. One of the officers demanded his identification. After examining it he was told that he was free to go. When the young man subsequently asked for the officer's identification however, the officer quickly changed his mind and said, "Let's take you to jail instead."

A trespass charge filed against this male at the time of the arrest was dismissed after review of the video. After an internal investigation, the city's independent police monitor stated that the officer would receive a "fair punishment" but refused to say what that punishment was. The ACLU filed a lawsuit on the young man's behalf. After months of negotiations the city agreed to pay him $8,500. The Denver Police Department has since issued a training bulletin to all officers, stating that: "No retaliatory action shall be taken against any member of the community based on the request for identification."

CASE STUDY:
Not their finest hour

On March 16, 2010, Mark Allise was walking his two dogs on the streets of Denver, Colorado, when he saw a police officer pull over a driver who had run a stop sign. Allise, claiming that he saw the man stop at the stop sign, approached the police car to volunteer information and to appear in court about the incident. He claims that the officer "didn't like it at all" and asked for his ID, which he provided. Afterwards, another police officer arrived on scene and Allise, who claims he was nervous, began taking photos of the two officers on his cell phone.

In the surveillance video released by the city and county, a police officer appears to hand Allise back his ID and a piece of paper after which Allise pulls out his cell phone to photograph the two officers. The two officers approach him again and one of the officers grabs his hand in an attempt to get the cell phone. The other officer also tries to help restrain him. In the ensuing struggle Allise tries to spin away from the officers and is thrust into a guardrail by the officers. One officer appears to strike him with his knee and punches him several times. Eventually, the two officers gain control and are able to handcuff him. After the incident, Allise was taken to the hospital where he was treated for a cut on his eye and a concussion.

Allise's attorney claimed that his client was arrested on the nonexistent charge of photographing a cop. The city agreed to pay a $35,000 settlement to him. Both officers were suspended and docked several days' pay.

In the chapter dealing with police misconduct, we briefly discussed having police officers wear a microphone and record all duty related conversations. Surely doing so would, to a large degree, eliminate many of these types of complaints because officers would refrain from engaging in the unprofessional and reactionary type of comments that lead to unsupportable or indefensible actions.

DEPARTMENTAL INTERACTION

Recruits should receive substantial instruction and guidance in this regard. They must be made aware of policies and procedures dealing with interactions between colleagues and supervisors. They must understand what is not tolerated or accepted, what action they can take if they experience or witness inappropriate behavior and what the consequences are of acting inappropriately themselves.

They should be made aware of the differences between bullying, sexual harassment and gender bias. They should also understand the difference between abusive behavior and legitimate criticism or supervision. They should learn to make every effort to resolve issues informally, when possible, and what they can do if that is not possible. And they should learn to analyze all of the information, including their own strengths and weakness, in an honest and dispassionate manner, before making any formal complaint.

Again, the predominant message is to treat colleagues in a professional, dignified and respectful manner, to be vigilant against permitting or taking part in inappropriate behavior and to be tolerant of the different personalities of colleagues and supervisors.

20

TRUTH VS. LAW —
THE CRIMINAL JUSTICE SYSTEM

Enter not these doors seeking justice, for this citizen,
is a House of the Law!

For all of its many faults, the justice system generally gets it right where it counts. That is, it rarely convicts an innocent person and usually convicts the guilty. Like the police, the justice system is often the victim of public misconception with many people believing that far fewer guilty people are convicted than is actually the case. In fact, the conviction rate or percentage in North America is very high, averaging at about 60% – 70%.

In North America, the government makes the laws, the police enforce them and the court system determines guilt *based on the application of those laws.* It's important to understand that distinction. The courts do not simply try to determine guilt or innocence based on evidence. They also determine if the proper process was followed in making and enforcing the law. That is why the courts are not so much about truth and justice, as most people would consider it, but about the law. That is precisely why a guilty person may well go free in spite of overwhelming evidence if the court determines that the law has not been properly applied.

There are any number of things that can affect this. Some are very technical in nature and may only be understood by someone versed in the law. Some involve the validity of the law itself. Or whether it was properly crafted or breaches some aspect of human rights, or is in conflict with some other law or legislation. Some involve police or prosecutorial errors or procedures such as improper seizure of evidence, unlawful arrests, failure to read suspects their rights, improperly obtained confessions, abuse of authority or process and many others.

It's often difficult for a lay person to understand how a suspect might give a complete confession and still be acquitted. Or how a weapon with the suspect's fingerprints or DNA might not be allowed as evidence. In truth, it's often hard for police officers and prosecutors to understand it too.

The criminal system has become so complicated and technical that it has impacted significantly on police resources. What used to be a two-page search warrant has grown to 20 pages. Twenty page affidavits are now 50. Disclosure requirements alone add days and weeks to the time it takes to prepare a major file for court. An impaired driving case that used to take one or two hours can now take five or six hours. What this means is that officers are required to have a higher degree of legal and technological knowledge and must spend more time on administrative functions than ever before.

Police departments wishing to maintain the same patrol or street coverage require additional officers, and this frequently conflicts with the need of governments to maintain or even reduce police budgets. At some point, costs and budgets have to be controlled. This will require considerable change in how many departments operate and what services they can or can't provide. It will also require an assessment of how they integrate with other parts of the justice system. In this regard, the court system itself may have to contemplate some changes.

If one considers that the justice system is of and for the people and funded by the people, then it's amazing how little it is operated for the people! Court hours tend to be Monday to Friday from 9 AM to 4:30 PM with little regard for when the public and police are available.

RECOMMENDED REFORMS

With so many of the public working during those times, and with police officers on different shifts, it would make considerable sense to have some courts open and available during the afternoon and evening hours. It would allow civilian witnesses to attend court without losing time from work. It would also allow officers on afternoon and evening shifts to attend court without incurring overtime and without sacrificing sleep time or days off.

In fact, other than requiring judges and court staff to work some shift work, there doesn't seem to be any negatives and there are several positives. Surely it would not be difficult to impose, and even if current judges and staff were exempt by contract, all new hires and judicial appointments could be required to do so.

Some evidence that is given in court by officers is strictly technical in nature. This might include laboratory results, fingerprint results, photographs, measurements and a host of other objective, measurable results and examinations. Would it be possible for the courts to allow some of this type of evidence to be given via sworn affidavit as opposed to personal court appearances? The officer could provide the court and defense counsel with the evidence they would be giving, and barring a challenge by defense, the court could accept the affidavit as evidence.

With the advances in technology, could officers, in some

cases, give evidence via video conferencing? Could judges sign search warrants and other legal documents using electronic signatures via email? These are certainly legal and accepted practices in the business world. It would certainly and considerably reduce the ever expanding demand on police resources.

These are just a few thoughts and suggestions about how the current court system could be changed in order to integrate more efficiently with police operations and ultimately provide a superior and more cost effective justice system. Regardless, we can no longer rely on doing things a certain way because that's just the way it's always been done. The justice system is always slow to change. But change it must!

21

THE POLICE WISH LIST

Were I but king for a day. Oh what changes
I could make — what havoc I might wreak.

I suspect that most people, at one time or another, have wondered what they would do if they were ever put in control, made the boss, the president or even. . .the king! Well, this is my version of that very thing. My wish list!

While there is no doubt this entire chapter is a bit tongue in cheek, there is also a bit of real wishful thinking. Certainly there are a number of things that I would have loved to see as a police officer and which would, in my opinion, be of great value today. I understand that these are simply pie in the sky dreams and are virtually guaranteed to never happen, but let me have some fun anyway. . .play Devil's advocate if you will!

"THREE STRIKES" LAW

An incredible amount of police and justice system time is spent dealing with the same offenders time and time again. Many of these offenders have records spanning years with multiple convictions. I would love to see a Three Strikes Law, but a different version of the one that has received so much criticism in California. There, a suspect convicted for the third offence receives a mandatory life sentence regardless of the seriousness of the third or prior offences.

The version I'd like to see, would require that any person convicted of a third or subsequent offence be sentenced to the maximum allowable time for the offence that was committed. For example, if a third conviction happened to be for an offence with a maximum sentence of two years then they would receive two years. If it was 15 years they would get 15 years.

It would be hard to argue that this was cruel and unusual punishment. Maximum sentences are mandated by the law as passed by government. Would a multiple offender not fit the requirements for receiving a maximum sentence? If not, then who would?

I believe this would prevent much of the crime in many areas. It would certainly go a long way to removing chronic offenders from society and it would free police resources which could be targeted towards other areas.

FIREARMS LAW

If an offender uses or is in possession of a firearm during the commission of another offence, they should receive a mandatory 10 year sentence. It should be served consecutively to any other sentence they may receive and the courts should not be allowed to factor that 10-year sentence into any other sentence than might normally be imposed.

For example, if a suspect used a firearm to commit an armed robbery, they might normally receive a five-year sentence for the actual armed robbery. This law would mean that upon completion of that five-year sentence, the prisoner would begin the mandatory 10-year sentence.

Many of the experts (read defense lawyers) will argue and say that it is too punitive and will not reduce firearm crimes. I disagree. But regardless, at least those convicted under this law would be out of circulation and pose no threat to the public for at least 10 years! I'd call that a win.

SECURE DRUG AND ALCOHOL REHAB FACILITIES

Much of the crime that is committed, and the police resources necessary to respond to it, are as a result of people who have substance abuse problems. While many prefer to call and deal with this as a medical problem, in reality it is both a medical problem and a policing problem.

Regardless of how and why they are addicted, many use crime as the way to pay for their drugs or alcohol. As a result, they often end up being dealt with by the police and the justice system. Not surprisingly, neither is particularly well suited to handle this type of problem.

As we have seen before, the people who tend to fall through society's cracks typically become a problem or responsibility of the police. That of course means that people who may need crisis intervention, medical treatment or counseling services wind up being dealt with by police. Since they are woefully ill equipped to do so, it leads to a wide variety of problems for both the individual and the police.

I wonder what would happen if the different levels of government, perhaps in conjunction with private businesses such as insurance companies, were to build secure rehab facilities? They would be staffed with a combination of security personnel, medical personnel and various professional counselors and educators.

With secure facilities, the addict would be forced to stay for the duration of the program and this alone might have very positive results. Many addicts enter voluntary rehab and then leave before completion. There are doubtless many reasons why they leave, but the fact remains that when they depart early, the program is ineffective and the addict is back on the street committing crimes again.

If the court determined that an offender was addicted to drugs or alcohol, they could be sentenced to a specific time in this facility for mandatory rehab. If, upon release, a person continued to commit criminal acts, was a chronic re-offender, resisted treatment or failed to respond in spite of the rehab, they should be considered an ongoing threat to society. In such a case, they should be sent to the secure rehab facility until medically detoxed and then sent to prison or some other form of detention to serve whatever sentence the court imposed.

At least with this system, the courts would have options that they just do not have today. And one has to consider that at least some, if not many, of these people would respond well to the rehab and successfully integrate back into society.

SECURE MENTAL HEALTH FACILITIES

When it comes to mental health, it is most definitely not an individual's fault that they are suffering from a mental illness. Certainly there are some however, who refuse to take medication that would help them or who intensify the problem by using alcohol or drugs. From a *medical* point of view, the real concern is to treat the illness in the best way possible. But from a *policing* point of view, the concerns are much different.

While a great amount of sympathy might be extended to a person suffering a mental illness, a police officer has to react to the behavior of an individual, often with little concern, or even knowledge, of what the causal factors are. In fact, studies have shown that if a subject is unable to engage the police in normal or logical conversation, the odds of a violent confrontation increase substantially.

If a person is armed with a weapon and threatening others, it requires immediate police action. Even if it were known that the person was mentally ill, it would likely have little bearing on the officer's response. No officer wants to hurt or kill a mentally ill person, but the fact remains that they are just as capable of causing serious injury or death as anyone else.

Even if nonviolent, the mentally ill can require a disproportionate amount of police time and resources. Surely there should be some secure facility where the courts could send a mentally ill person who required close monitoring, treatment, medical care or proper nourishment. Without question, it would be preferable to having them live on the streets, being victimized and with no serious chance to get well.

It should not fall to the police or the courts to be dealing with these issues. The simple fact is that any financial saving gained by the closing of mental health facilities is simply passed on to operating costs of the courts, emergency rooms and police departments. *In the end, the public saving is low and the cost paid by the mentally ill is high.*

TRUTH-BASED JUSTICE SYSTEM

I would like to see the justice system move from a predominantly law based system to more of a truth based one. It seems to me that the perfect system would be where every guilty offender was found guilty and every innocent accused was acquitted.

If one believes that the justice system exists for the benefit of society, then society should be responsible for that system. Laws should be such, that they balance the individual's rights and freedoms with society's right to safety and security.

In this sort of system, the goal would be to determine the truth, and considerable latitude should be allowed. For example, the measure of an acceptable confession would be, is it a true confession or is it a false confession? In other words, was it coerced in a manner that would cause any reasonable, normal person to falsely confess?

Why should the police, the very ones who are attempting to solve the crime, be forced to provide a police warning which literally advises the person not to tell the truth. Would it not be more appropriate if every citizen, including those suspected in a crime, was required to answer truthfully to any question asked by the police in the official conduct of their duties?

To date, nobody has ever really explained to me, in any satisfactory manner, why a suspect should have the right to silence? I know it has been a basic enshrined right for many years and seems to have originated in ancient English common law, but I don't know exactly what it's based on? Did it evolve from an era when torture was used to question prisoners? If so, should we not revisit the issue now that it's the 21st century? It's curious that the legal system is almost the only place where this right to silence exists.

Certainly, we raise and expect our children to be honest and to tell the truth even when it means confessing to some act or behavior. Schools and universities expect students to tell the truth about all matters they are questioned about. Most businesses would demand explanations from employees who had been accused of some wrong doing. Lying or failing to tell the truth on resumes is almost always actionable.

If someone accidently damaged a car in a parking lot, the law and social etiquette demand that they leave their name and contact information. Insurance companies can deny claims if a client lies or refuses to provide truthful answers. We expect truthful explanations from friends, spouses, co-workers and public officials for events which may raise questions. In fact, in almost all cases excepting the criminal justice system, we demand and expect that culpable people will take responsibility for what they have said or done. What an intriguing topic for a scholarly debate one day.

Certainly I am not advocating that we abandon all individual rights, or move towards a police state. In fact, doing so would be counter-productive to determining the truth. There should always be due process. Police should still need to follow procedures, obtain court orders and respect the law. But should it not be every citizen's duty to assist in maintaining law and order?

The question is whether evidence which clearly points to the truth should be discarded because of a procedural or technical error? Should a true confession be disallowed because the accused didn't fully understand his rights? Shouldn't the real legal test be *"will this confession or evidence assist the court in determining the truth"*?

Yes, I do feel that more focus on truth and less on law would be a positive step and one that could be achieved within the rule of law. As it is now, it often feels as if crime and the justice system is simply a big legal game, with rules put in place to make it fair for everyone. Do we really want it to be fair to the people who are victimizing us? Is it really a game at all?

POLICE SERVICES

Most police departments address the issue of budgets and services on a regular basis. There is a continual challenge to provide maximum service for minimal cost and in this regard it is not all that different from private business. Where it does differ is that police departments are not as in control of their costs as most businesses.

If a major crime occurs, the police must deal with it. If there is a riot, a VIP visit or some other unforeseen event, police have no real opportunity to allow for it in their budget. When the government closes a mental health facility, the police will be forced to commit many resources to the social problems that will create. In a world where the public has no appetite for increased taxes, but continues to heap additional responsibilities onto the police, some action will have to be taken.

The hard question is determining what services can be stopped or reduced and which should not. Is it cost effective to have a fully trained officer attend minor property crimes, building alarms or other incidents that might require little more than the taking of a report? Could departments hire retired police officers at a substantially reduced salary to assume those types of duties?

Do we need fully trained officers to handle routine traffic accidents and minor enforcement duties or could this be handed over to others? Can departments afford to have units like community relations or school liaison? Can they afford not to?

Are we close to the point where there will be two levels of police officers? One being a lower paid level which deals with all minor, non-violent, property type crime and one a fully trained, higher paid level that deals with everything else?

As mentioned earlier, could we make better use of recently retired police officers who may still wish to continue working and are already trained and knowledgeable?

CIVIL LIBERTIES UNIONS

One of the most vocal critics of the police are the various civil liberties organizations. Where I live, it's the BC Civil Liberties Union. This group continually complains and bleats on about how the police conduct their duties. They are especially critical of those cases where police investigate allegations of police wrong doing. They call it a conflict of interest, an abuse of process and in almost every case, accuse police of covering up.

I find it beyond hypocritical that they take this position when they are members of the legal system which has the most incestuous conflict of interest on earth!

If a lawyer misbehaves, they are investigated and disciplined by other lawyers (the Law Society). If they are criminally charged, the charge must be approved by a lawyer (the prosecutor). If approved, they are prosecuted by a lawyer, judged by a lawyer and sentenced by a lawyer. If they appeal, their case is reviewed by a panel of lawyers, right up to and including the Supreme Court, which is comprised of lawyers.

Can you imagine the hair pulling and veritable frothing at the mouth if police officers had to have charges against them approved by another police officer? If the prosecutor was a police officer? How about if the judge was a police officer and all appeals were heard by a panel of police officers? Well, that is exactly the situation in the legal system!

The sheer arrogance of these groups is almost overwhelming. I suppose, in their defense, they must truly feel that lawyers have so much higher moral and ethical standards than the rest of us that they and they alone are capable of policing and judging themselves without any conflict of interest??

It must be clearly stated that these civil liberties unions are stand-alone groups and certainly do not reflect the views and opinions of all or even most lawyers.

I'd like to see these civil liberties unions and groups take a look at their own organization and have the courage to take the same stance against the legal system as they have against the police. Demand that lawyers who are charged criminally must not have charges approved by another lawyer but by an outside agency. If charges are approved, they must demand that lawyers not be judged by other lawyers but by someone outside of the legal system. If they appeal, they should demand that appeals be heard and reviewed by someone other than a lawyer/judge.

If they don't do this, then they are simply another self serving, hypocritical, do as I say not what I do type of organization that already has zero credibility in the police world and should have none anywhere else!

Interesting points for discussion! Obviously there will be many who heartily disagree with much or all of the comments made in the wish list and I understand that. I've tried not to take myself too seriously with this chapter. Sometimes though, big change begins with a small idea.

CONCLUSION

Law enforcement is an honorable career and the vast majority of the men and women who work in law enforcement are honorable people.

This has been my humble attempt to provide you with a glimpse into the world of policing. To help you understand that world a little bit better, and to introduce you to the faces Behind the Badge.

It was my great honor to be a member of the Royal Canadian Mounted Police and to take my place amongst the many outstanding men and women who have and are currently serving.

It bears repeating when I state that law enforcement is an honorable career and the vast majority of the men and women who are law enforcement officers are honorable people. I believe that honestly and absolutely. The point I have tried to make is that they are human beings. . .no more and no less.

There is simply no way to avoid the fact that every police organization will have its share of personnel and operational problems, its public relations disasters and its internal disputes. That is inevitable. How they respond to those issues and deal with the problems is what will define them.

So perhaps it's time to stop focusing on particular police departments and focus on police work itself. Are we asking too much of these young men and women? Is it realistic to hold them to standards so high they are virtually impossible to meet? What is a "fair" standard? How can that be determined? Certainly by men and women smarter than me.

But if we want our best and our brightest to serve as police officers, we have to find a way to treat them better. To accept that in spite of best efforts, mistakes will be made, and that some mistakes will have a high cost.

We must try to understand and forgive those mistakes and be vigilant against focusing on the relatively few failures and ignoring the many successes...from allowing the bad conduct of a few to taint the exceptional work of the many. Perhaps we should consider this:

Is it possible that no human being is really and truly equipped to handle all of the things a police officer must see, do and feel on a regular basis throughout their career and that ultimately, individuals and organizations can only do their best?

It's not hard to be a critic. All you require is an opinion. The challenge is in becoming an informed critic. So, if you are a critic and feel that you could do better, please, step up and be fitted for a uniform...when you have faced the challenges and passed the test then by all means, weigh in, criticize, offer suggestions and judgments. At least you will have earned the right.

Works Cited

Bernstein, M. 2009. "Chief Recommends Sergeant's Suspension in Chasse's Death." The Oregonian, Portland. September 23.

Brown, T.R., Beutler, L.E., Nussbaum, P.D. & Keith, M.E. "Changing personality patterns of police officers." *Professional Psychology: Research and Practice.* 19.5 (1988): 503-507. Print.

Charlotte-Mecklenburg Police Department. 2001. Directive 100-104: Discipline Philosophy. Interactive Directives Guide. Charlotte, N.C.: Charlotte-Mecklenburg Police Department.

Health Canada. Canadian Medical Association. *Health Care in Canada* 2004. Print.

Laur, D.A. "Edged Weapons Tactics & Counter Tactics." *LWC Books.* Web. October 2012. <www.lwcbooks.com>.

MacAlister, D. "Police Involved Deaths: The Failure of Self Investigation: Final Report." *bccla.org.* BC Civil Liberties Association. Web. <http://bccla.org/wp-content/uploads/2012/05/20101123-McAllister-Report-Police-Involved-Deaths-The-Failure-of-Self-Investigation.pdf>.

McQuaid, M. "Vancouver." *Province Newspaper* 2012, n. pag. Print.

Pitkin, J. 2009. "Chasse Cop Christopher Humphreys Placed on Administrative Leave." Wilamette Week Online. November 19 (accessed May 10, 2010).

Remsberg, D.A. "Surviving Edged Weapons." (2012. *Real Self-Defense.* Web. October 2012. <www.real-self-defense.com>.

Seagan, S. "What Is Excessive Force?." 14 July 1999. Web. 2012. <http://abcnews.go.com/US/story?id=96509&page=1>.

Siddle, B. International Association of Law Enforcement Firearms Instructors. *Critical Incident Amnesia.* 2001. Print.

Stephens, D.W., *Police Discipline: A Case for Change,* Washington, D.C.: U.S. Department of Justice, National Institute of Justice, 2011.

Surette, R. *Media, Crime, and Criminal Justice: Images and Realities 2nd Edition.* 1998. Print.

Torpy, B. 2009. "In Atlanta, It Can Be a Long Wait for Cases to Be Resolved." The Atlanta Journal-Constitution. August 1.

Tueller, D. "How Close is Too Close?." *S.W.A.T. Magazine.* Mar 1983: n. page. Print.

U.S. Justice. National Institute of Justice. *Police Use of Force.* 1999. Print.

U.S. Justice. National Institute of Justice.*Research Report - Police Use of Force.* 1999. Print.

Index

About the Author

Wayne grew up in rural Saskatchewan and wrote his first letter to the Royal Canadian Mounted Police (RCMP) when he was 13 years old. Upon finishing high school, he attended the University of Saskatchewan, graduating with a Bachelor of Arts degree in 1975. That same year he joined the RCMP.

Wayne spent the five years in uniform patrol duties on Vancouver Island. In 1981 he was transferred to northern duties in Prince Rupert, B.C. where he spent one year in uniform patrol duties before transferring to the plain clothes GIS (Detective) section. It was there that he had his first real experience investigating homicides and major crimes and from that point he knew what he wanted to do as a police officer.

In 1985, Wayne asked for and was granted a transfer to Surrey, B.C. which was and still is the largest RCMP detachment in Canada. His reasoning was simple. He was fascinated and intrigued by the demands and challenges of major criminal investigations and Surrey offered the best opportunities. Subsequently, he was transferred to the Surrey Serious Crimes Unit and went on to spend the next 10 years investigating the type of major crimes that occur in large, urban centers.

He took part in over 80 homicide investigations, many as the main investigator and many as one of the peripheral investigators.

In 1988 Wayne became one of two Hostage Negotiators at Surrey Detachment and went on to work with the Emergency Response Team on many hostage and barricaded persons investigations. Also in 1988 he was promoted to Corporal.

In 1995 Wayne was promoted to the rank of Sergeant but his focus had changed and he knew that he needed a change too. In 1996, with many reservations and a heavy heart, he resigned from the RCMP and immediately began a new career in real estate.

To date, Wayne has maintained many friendships with current and retired RCMP members and is a member of the RCMP Veterans' Association. He remains proud beyond words of his career in law enforcement.

Wayne currently makes his home in Surrey, B.C. where he spends time with his wife, two married children and five wonderful grandchildren.

Wayne can be contacted at ryans@telus.net.